ABANDON
BRANDON

BY

BRANDON J MCDERMOTT

FOREWORD BY OTIS XII

CONTENTS

A big thank you to the many people along the way who've helped me write this book. From those who heard my story many years ago and told me to tell it, to the surrogates and mentors who pushed me to be the man I am today. This list includes, but is not limited to: My first foster mom Pat, Cheri Zagurski (for more than you know), Mrs. Tonnies, Shaun Behrens (Mr. B) and Mr. Earnhardt for being the teachers I needed. Thanks to M. Leigh Hood for the countless hours of edits and patience.

To my wife, my heart, who keeps me on the straight and narrow and loves me despite my shortcomings.

And finally, thank you to those who believed in me, and more importantly those who didn't.

FOREWORD

This is Brandon's story.

It is not an easy story to tell, and it is not an easy story to read. If you are seeking comfort in his story, you may not find it easily. You will have to be brave. If you are looking for inspiration, you may not find it here without effort. You will have to bring your own faith to the journey.

I realize that a note such as this should be welcoming. I should give you a sense of what's coming and encourage you to be excited about what is ahead of you as a reader. The thing is, in the case of a book like this, I have to warn you. There is some very rough stuff in Brandon's story. It's a book about personal triumph, but it's also a grinding tale of simple survival. If you want to share in his victory, you will have to subject yourself to some of the pain.

I myself am a survivor of sexual and physical abuse, maybe you are too, that said, our stories are not his. We survivors share some level of mutual understanding, but we do not know, really know the truth of each person's experience. Our own individual memories may have led us in completely different directions as we sought our own healing. We all may share a diagnosis, but that does not mean we are all alike.

Emotional and sexual abuse is an attack on the very center of our beings. It rips, tears, burns, and dissolves the very soul of the victim. The result of the abuse gets survivors the diagnosis of PTSD - Post Traumatic Stress Disorder. The tag is misleading; there is no "Post" about it. The truth is, it never ends.

Our stories and Brandon's story share one central reality, they do not end. All of us have been changed. Transformed - some for good - some for ill. Trauma is eternal. The salvation we seek is some way to transform that trauma. We seek an answer for changing the destructive energy into healing. And that answer, it seems to me, is unique to each of us.

Brandon's story is brutal and heartbreaking. It is upsetting and disturbing on a primal level. I can promise you it will grab you and stay with you a very long time. I cannot promise you that you will be inspired or gain any insight. There are those who tell me I should offer a "trigger warning," and perhaps I should. To discover new truths, to learn new ways of seeing, requires that a few triggers be pulled.

I wish you love and peace in your own story. Read on and be kind along the way - kind to yourself as you share in some hard and difficult events, and kind to the kid who's sharing them.

This is Brandon's story.

Written by Douglas Wesselmann "Otis XII"

Chapter 1 – Normalcy

I was baptized in my mother's blood.

Some kids have a baptism ceremony with extended family – grandparents, god parents, aunts and uncles. They take pictures, share food, and make memories. There was no food at my baptism. No one took pictures. But the impact is lasting.

I was three-years-old and my mother came home in a hurry. My dad and I were the only ones there. The door slammed behind her.

"Hey, I'm going to grab a few dollars…" my mother said as she passed my father on the way to the bedroom.

"For what?" my father yelled, watching an episode of *Sanford and Son* on TV while I played with my Ninja Turtles on the ground in front of him.

"We want to get a bag for later," she responded. "He's going to pay us back later."

His ears perked up and he immediately got out of his seat. He threw the remote into the chair as he stomped back towards the bedroom. I was scared, but I got up and followed him. I could hear him yelling at her down the hall. When I got back there, standing by the open door, mom had found dad's wallet underneath a heap of dirty clothes. She rifled through it, alternating between counting bills and trying to explain the situation to my dad. I could see my father's temper building. No one was going to smoke all his money away.

"The fuck you are!"

He ran over to her, reaching for the money. I could see mom was scared, she stared at him, her eyes wide open. She wasn't sure of what he would do. Dad grabbed her. They began to wrestle over the money. She tried holding the cash in her hands and between her legs, where he couldn't get it. He poked and prodded her to get the money. I ran over to them, scared for my mom. Between their wrestling, I could hear cars passing on the street through the open windows. Outside, the world went on, but inside, my world was being shaped, my mind molded.

"What are you doing?" my mother asked helplessly.

"You're not going to steal my fucking money, whore! Not for some drugs for your fucking loser brother," my dad shot back.

Dad used to do drugs, too. But after he quit it all, he was "above it."

Mom briefly escaped dad's grasp. She tried to make a run for the door. This only angered him. He chased her down.

After his attempts to pry the money from her hands failed, he slammed my mother against the wall, looked her square in the eye and head-butted her. There was a loud crack. By this time, I was standing under my mom crying. She let out a guttural yelp as blood poured from her nose and onto me, her three-year-old son. The money fell to the ground, covered in blood. I stood underneath her as she bawled. Her blood continued to spill. She consoled me, her nose clearly out of place.

My father didn't comfort my mother, who cried as he walked away. He was a proud victor in that moment, getting what he wanted, proving the point he wanted to prove. He trash-talked her as she tried to clean up her mess. It was her mess. He made it so.

"Clean that shit up! You're getting blood all over the fucking carpet! Look at your son, he's covered in your blood. Go get a towel!"

Frantically, my mother tried to clean me up. She didn't realize she needed to stop her nose from bleeding first. She was in shock, trying to wipe up the blood with her bare hands as it pooled beneath us. I was wet with my mother's blood, it was in my eyes, on my face and it stained my clothes. It smelled bad.

Watching dad hit mom wasn't new to me, but it still was never easy to watch. At three-years-old, they were both my world. They were all I knew. In many ways, this was my coming of age. One of the very first, and most intense, memories I have. It was the birth of what would be my childhood.

This was my baptism into the world of my dad. The way he treated, used and abused people he claimed to love and care for was just a portion of his depravity. I had no idea that this wasn't normal. It was a distorted example of what a "father" was.

***

My mom tells the story this way. My parents met in 1985. My aunt shopped at the local Hinky Dinky, a popular grocery store chain in Omaha at the time. She ran back home to tell my mother about the two "handsome guys," she met. One of them was a guy named Rick and the other my future dad. My aunt and mother went back to the store and found my dad and Rick waiting like two cool dudes, in a parked car, smoking cigarettes. Dad always thought he was the cool guy.

My aunt and Rick started what was a hot and heavy – but brief – love affair that night. It ended unceremoniously with my aunt catching crabs and breaking up with him.

My mother and father hit it off and things progressed a bit slower than my aunt and Rick. Most relationships start off with a spark. The future is bright, and love's glow can be blinding. Same with my parents. My mom and dad weren't together for very long. They met in 1985, had me in '86 and Brittney in '87. Then they got married in November of 1989 and had my youngest sister in 1990. But by 1992, any reason either of them had for staying together was overcome by a poisonous desire to hurt each other.

3

My father ran our trailer just like he ran his marriage, into the ground. I'd later come to find out this was his blueprint for everything good in his life. To grab it, suck the life out of it and spit it out when it was ready to be discarded.

I spent much of my childhood, before they divorced, watching my dad humiliate my mother. He called her names, picked on her for arbitrary things and put her down in front of my sisters and me. Most of the time it seemed like it was just out of sheer boredom. We were just tools in his game.

"You're so fat, why don't you walk more?" he said to mom. "Brandon, look at your mom's fat ass. Look how big that is. It's big like a hippo, isn't it?"

I was very young and wanted my dad's approval, so I agreed.

"Yeah, dad, it's like a hippo!" I said.

My dad laughed, seeing my mother was humiliated.

"Why are you doing this?" she asked on the verge of tears.

Then he told me, four-years-old at the time, to run full speed at my mother like a charging bull – headfirst – when she was turned the other way folding clothes. Seeking his acceptance and trusting his advice, I ran full-bore and hit my head in the middle of her behind – BANG! My father laughed, enraging my mother. Her humiliation turned to anger; she focused that rage at me, "correcting" her son for what he did wrong. She pushed me to the ground, and I started crying. My dad laughed louder. Of course, she couldn't correct my father.

Dad also liked to put mom down in front of other people, whether it was his parents or friends.

"You really are the stupidest person I know," he would say to her. "Use your fucking brain, you dumb bitch!"

Verbally abusing my mom showcased his control, like it was a skill. He really enjoyed this skill. One time the two of them decided to take Polaroid photos of each other naked. That isn't too abnormal, intimate couples taking naked photos of each other. But my father took these photos of my mother, his wife, and he showed them to his friends. Those friends told her. As an adult, I imagine the shame she must have felt, seeing the man she loved embarrass her. My father reveled in his malevolence. He may have gained some sexual pleasure from using my mother's trust and seeing it turn to dust. But it went much deeper; he found joy in seeing other's pain, especially in those he claimed to love.

I can't fathom doing any of this to someone I love, especially in front of my children. It deeply hurt my mother. It hurt her in the moment and for years to come. The same went for my sisters and me. Witnessing something like this at an early age, from someone who shapes and molds you, has a deep impact. It took years to wade through the abuse and it's after effects, to separate who I was from what dad did to me.

My father reigned over my mother in all ways: physically, emotionally and psychologically. My father didn't show affection to her with usual customs. He didn't dote on her, kiss her cheek or forehead. Instead, he'd demean her for being overweight, put her down for wearing bad clothes, for the trailer being dirty. Sometimes he'd run up behind her and tug on her breasts, whistling in front of my sisters and me. In some twisted way, this was normal for him. This was capital.

It became a game of hoping the abuse wouldn't happen to you. But also hoping not to watch your mother or sisters experience his abuse. After they divorced, it was almost a relief knowing he wouldn't hurt her anymore. I know now that when they split, it was the best thing that could've happened to her. She had a shot at a real life. He didn't get that memo and found new and inventive ways to hurt her, mostly through us. But now instead of being bystanders to his abuse, we were pawns in his schemes. It was my normalcy.

Chapter 2 – Just A Game

My father was very good at what he called "being aware of your surroundings." I think his anxiety gave him this talent. It stemmed from years of being bullied, being a bully, and drug use. He tried passing this trait on to me and my sisters. He knew if he was going to be in a room with other people, he needed some solace from the heavy feeling that anxiety brought. This gave him power. So, he always monitored what was happening around him and how others' feelings or moods were changing.

He always sensed when I was scared. He used the character "Zelda" from the horror movie *Pet Semetary,* to frighten me for several weeks after he made me watch it. He waited until night, until we were alone or in my grandparent's basement to spook me. He screamed like a banshee, shut the lights off and chased me in the dark. When I found a corner to hide in, behind some boxes or under a table, he ran upstairs and lock the door.

"Hahaha! You're never getting out. You live down there now! You're going to die today, boy. Time's up!"

He banged on the door several times, screaming. I ran to the top of the stairs, on the other side of the locked basement door.

"Let me out daddy! Please!" I pleaded with him.

I was terrified. My back was to the door, facing the bottom of the stairs and the dark basement.

"You're never getting out! Don't look at the bottom of the stairs, Zelda is coming to get you!"

I was in tears. He got his score – what he was looking for all along – the exhilaration of scaring me, seeing me helpless. Then he carried on like nothing happened, until he found someone or something else to use.

He enjoyed mentally tormenting us, his short temper always on display. He also enjoyed disparaging and mocking me for making simple mistakes. If I fumbled a plate or dropped something on the ground, he let out a big sigh of disgust.

"Boy, you're just as goddamned clumsy as your fucking mother," he said.

It was a way to remind you that you were less than him, that he was in control and you were nothing. Yet he was always quick to point to other kids that had it worse than me.

"You see that family down the block? he asked. "You should thank your lucky stars you aren't them."

There certainly was some twisted truth to that. Someone always has it worse. My father reminded us, all throughout our childhood how much better the McDermott family was — his family — than my mother's family. They were "trash." His mother and father, our paternal grandparents, loved us and he made sure to take advantage of his parent's nurturing. He benefited from their love for us. They loved us, so in turn, he did too. That way, indirectly, he could claim to be a "good dad."

***

There were times I deserved to be punished — when picking on my little sisters, being a destructive little boy, or failing to following directions. Then there were times like when we visited Grandpa's house in 1998. It was a frigid February day; the wind was so cold it crystalized my snot when I inhaled. Dad and I had gone to the grocery store in Florence for a few things. I remember my grandfather was out with Grandma at a doctor's appointment when we got back to the house. He wanted my dad to pick up all the fixings for his family-famous spaghetti. I was looking forward to dinner that night. There were sure to be the large pieces of spicy Italian sausage, onions, peppers and the best garlic bread I've ever had. The way he got the garlic toast to stay buttery and soft is something I'll never understand.

We got back and put the food away in the basement. We had just finished stacking cans of tomatoes, when my dad spotted an unwound extension cord on the ground.

He knelt to pick up the cord, pushing aside an empty plastic bucket and a couple cans of paint. He looked up at me. I stood there frozen, wondering what he was doing. The next moment, it hit me. I knew what was going down.

"You've got ten seconds to run and hide," he said with a twisted smile.

I felt a lump in my throat and my heartbeat speed up. Without question, I took off upstairs. About half-way up, ideas of where to hide came to my mind. Could I hide behind the bar in the living-room? No, it would make too much noise. Grandma was somewhat of a hoarder, being a child of the depression. She kept towers of old newspapers and magazines stacked up back there. He'd easily hear the crumpling papers. Could I make it to the back porch, or even to the backyard? Not without my coat and not without causing the heavy door to creak. What about under the kitchen table? No, he'd check there first. My next inkling was a decent one: under the dining room table.

It was a large table that could seat ten people, but its chairs were stacked with magazines, clothes and recyclables.

A long tablecloth hid most of the space underneath. Plus, the family Chihuahua liked to pee and poop there. She was the only one who could fit without trouble. A foot bar connected the table's legs about six inches above the ground. It crisscrossed underneath, so you could rest your feet as you sat. I thought I could stand on it, so dad wouldn't see me.

When I hit the top of the stairs, I knew exactly where to go.

8

"7….8….9…HERE I COME…" my dad exclaimed.

By the time I heard him clear the stairs I was already under the table, hidden as much as one could be in ten seconds. I could smell the pee and poop on the stained newspapers folded out to catch the excrement. The carpet underneath was sticky with old, caked urine. I tried to keep my breaths slow and shallow, so he wouldn't hear me, and I wouldn't get sick from the stench.

He ran to the living room first and checked behind the couch and the bar. I knew that was a bad idea. I was safe. He ran to the kitchen, the first-floor bathroom. I wasn't anywhere to be found. He came back to the dining room and stood still. I could see the extension cord dangling by his feet. He let out an ominous laugh. I shuddered, knowing it was only a matter of time. Grandma and Grandpa weren't going to be home in time to save me. He ran upstairs to check the bedrooms.

I thought, should I move? Maybe to a spot he's already checked? No that would make noise and tell him where I was. I'd better stay put. I was lucky enough up to that point.

After about two minutes, he marched down the stairs, each step calculated. I could feel it; he knew where I was. He got to the bottom and walked to the edge of the table. He ripped one of the chairs out of place. The newspapers stacked on the chair fell to the ground. He pulled the tablecloth up and stuck his face down. He smiled like a movie villain.

"I've found you, boy," he said, me by the arm and throwing me on the ground.

WAP! WAP!

I let out a yelp.

"Daddy, stooooop, I didn't do anything wrong!" I yelled at him.

WAP!

My cries intensified. I couldn't even think of why I deserved this. I was being a good boy, I thought to myself, trying to shield my back. On the third swat my left hand caught a piece of the extension cord. Then he unwound it, and gripped the cord. The metal electrical connection hung loosely. I looked up at him, and he smiled at me.

"DADDY! NO!"

WAP!

I writhed in pain. He finally got his fill. He laughed as he picked me up and told me I was going to be okay. I limped as I walked to the bathroom to get tissues to wipe away the tears and blow my nose. He was still laughing like this was a game, a game I lost and a game I should've understood. I didn't. I think he knew time was up; grandma and grandpa would be home soon. He led me to the kitchen to coax me out of my crying with food. He made me some strawberry Toaster Strudels. Then we went to the living room and he put on *Cheech and Chong*. While he didn't do drugs anymore, he loved reminiscing about his drug days and *Cheech and Chong* was a part of that.

Perhaps this was planned all along and the extension cord was just the random tool that he found in that moment.

That night, I looked at my back in the mirror. I could clearly see the three strikes from the wound-up cord and a big purple and red spot on my shoulder where the head of the extension cord hit me. It was cut open, surrounded by a bruise. It hurt when I touched it. My eyes began to well up with tears as I thought about what had happened.

From a young age, I felt special, like God was watching out for me, in some way, like God knew I was strong and was pushing me to be stronger. Dad's abuse, I felt, was a way to really test it.

***

My mother went to the store for groceries early on a spring day in 1992. She had been gone for quite some time. In my young mind, she could have been gone for half a day. But it's more likely it was just an hour or two. My dad and I were at the trailer in northwest Omaha my grandpa gave my dad as a wedding present. MTV was playing on the TV. The windows were open and the breeze wafted the cigarette-smoke stained curtains back and forth.

My dad loved watching music videos. He always kept MTV on for background noise. That is, if he wasn't blasting *For Unlawful Carnal Knowledge (F.U.C.K.)*, the latest Van Halen Album, on the stereo. That day Soul Asylum's "Runaway Train" was playing. Dad was only half watching the video on the TV as he read the *Omaha World Herald* sports section. My sisters were taking a nap in the backroom. I lucked out and didn't have to nap that day. Dad needed some company.

Dad began catching on to the fact I was worried and scared that mom has been for a long time.

"Your mom's not coming back," he said to me.

I looked at him puzzled, hoping he was wrong. He was sincere and shot straight at me.

"She's left for good, boy."

He savored my sadness, a bully sizing up its prey.

I was terrified. At five-years-old, the idea my mother was never coming back was too much to bear. My dad acted serious. Why would he lie about this? What he said was gospel, I thought. I was convinced that he was right.

He enjoyed every moment of my torment. He put down the newspaper and focused on upsetting me. "What are we going to do for dinner, now that Mom is dead?" he asked. "How am I going to find another wife?"

The simple, straight-to-the-point style of his comments hurt me deeply, and showed me he was being frank.

She did come back, groceries in tow, and I felt a weight release from my little chest.

Several years later, in the summer of 1999, this same scene was re-enacted, only this time with someone else – a child of a friend of dad's girlfriend. The kid was about two or three and severely mentally impaired. Dad was babysitting for his single mother. I do not recall this child's name.

My father's nastiness, when heated properly, stirred something in him. He had the gift of villainous creativity when he was angry but also when he was bored. My father decided to call the child he was watching "Alien Nation," a reference to a made-for-TV movie from the 1980s. It was a movie about race of aliens new to Earth trying to assimilate. Well, these aliens had over exaggerated heads and so, too, did this young kid. His head was very large, much bigger than a normal child his age, and he was top heavy. My dad enjoyed manipulating this kid into crying.

"Your mom is never coming back, buddy! She's dead! She's gone forever!" he said with glee.

A deep, wretched shriek came from the young child. The kid only wanted the one thing in the world familiar to him: his mother. Here was this grown man terrifying a mentally-disabled toddler for kicks.

To make matters worse, he egged me on to laugh at the boy. Slapping my back when he would cry, seeking my approval. This went on for several minutes until my father got his fix. Then he calmed the boy down with milk and ice cream. Finally, the cries gave way to soft whimpers and then to sighs. The child fell asleep from the emotional rollercoaster. Then I recalled my dad had done this same thing with me.

I dealt with my dad's beatings, because those wounds healed easier. Dad would always tire of hearing my cries and relent.

"Oh stop! It's not that bad, stop crying like a little girl. Don't be a faggot."

My father's physical abuse stung. But so did his emotional and psychological cruelty.

Chapter 3 – A Clumsy Break

When dad beat mom, he would usually corner and smother her, striking her once or twice to get his point across. My sister Brittney, who was a year younger than I, would always run and cower behind the recliner or couch.

But on one particular night, my mother simply had enough. It was November 1992, Christmas lights were strung up all over the trailer's living room. There were no gifts under the tree, but the Christmas tree was stood tall over everyone in the trailer like an impartial judge watching it all.

"Fuck you! You're not going to hurt me anymore!"

Dad had been on his normal tear, picking on my mother for being fat, lazy and not keeping the place clean. She ran to the kitchen, grabbed a butcher knife and started chasing my dad around the trailer.

My mother screamed, chasing my dad to their bedroom slashing at him. He ran around the waterbed in their bedroom to dodge her. She kept hacking at him wildly.

"What the fuck are you doing?" he screamed "You're going to put a hole in my fucking bed you stupid cunt!"

"MOMMY STOP!" my little sister Brittney yelled. Brittney and I followed mom to the bedroom when she got the knife.

"What are you fucking doing woman!" my father demanded, suddenly turning sensible and principled.

"I've had enough! You're not going to hurt me anymore!" my mother yelled.

I could see my mother having an epiphany right before my young eyes. Those years of abuse had piled up and she hit her limit. She knew what she needed to do. Not only was she planning to leave, she was going to take her kids with her.

"What, are you going to go live at your whore sister's house? They can't even write their own damn names! You've got nothing, sweetheart. You've got no place to stay. And you won't get these kids. They're mine!"

Mom eventually calmed down, thinking for herself again. Dad was angry, but he tried convincing her to stay. The trailer was still on edge, mom chain smoking cigarettes and watching out the window. She was looking for her sister, my aunt to pick her up. When my aunt showed up, dad accepted reality and his tone shifted again to putting mom down. Now he wanted her gone. She packed a small bag of clothes. That's all my dad allowed her to take. In a few short moments, she gave my two sisters hugs and kisses. She then turned to me and dejectedly hugged me. She told me to be strong. I didn't cry, but my sisters did. Mom left and my dad slammed the door, locking it behind him.

"She's going to regret leaving," he said.

He went to the kitchen window to watch her enter my aunt's car and drive away. That night, he paced back and forth yelling at my sisters and me for leaving our toys on the living room floor.

He spent the next few days calling friends, old girlfriends, and family – anyone who'd listen to him vent about my "whore mother."

"Listen to this shit..."– all the conversations seemed to begin the same way. He didn't want to be alone, and he wanted to get people on his side.

The story gets odder and murkier after that. Within weeks, my parents somehow agreed, that my mother would move back into the trailer. They agreed this was "the best thing for us kids." The holidays were just around the corner, and they wanted us to be together for Christmas.

The one caveat was that my mother and father were not together and my mother's boyfriend moved in with her. Additionally, my dad's lifelong alcoholic friend, Eddie, one of the twin brothers he grew up with, also moved in to our two-bedroom trailer. Eddie wasn't the cleanest person. We frequently found his pairs of jeans loaded with human feces. The man didn't wear underwear, and he didn't shower. He would just take off his dirty pants and hide them, often behind appliances, or under the bed – even under the trailer.

14

Any benefit from having two parents in the home was wiped out by having an unhygienic alcoholic lounging around and my mother's live-in boyfriend staying there too. I'm not sure how this arrangement came to be. Perhaps dad wanted my mother there, no matter how painful it was.

One morning my sister Brittney and I were eating cereal and watching cartoons. *James Bond Jr.* was on TV. It was a terrible cartoon, but we loved it. The show didn't last long, much like our living arrangement. We heard a commotion in the bedroom just feet away from the TV. She and I ran over to see what was going on, but the door was locked. Being the curious little kids we were, we knelt down to the bottom of the door. There was a one-inch crack and we peeked to see what was going on in the room. I saw my mother and her boyfriend fornicating. I had never seen anything like it. A sight to see at six-years-old. Brittney and I didn't know what to think at that moment. I remember we laughed, because we didn't know any better.

It was a confusing time to say the least. The trailer was filled with conflicting views and different people. It was a disorganized mess. Mom and Dad tried to keep the family together. To keep my sisters and I from feeling the effects of the divorce. What happened was worse. We lived in a strange universe while mom and dad acted like the world wasn't crashing around them. I didn't know who to trust, much less how to decipher what was happening.

Chapter 4 – Chip Off The Old Block

My parent's upbringing couldn't have been more dissimilar. Mom had only known abusive men. It played right into my father's desire for control. He wanted someone less than him – less smart, less affluent – and in his eyes – less of a person.

Her father was an alcoholic, a brick layer who beat her, her mother, and her siblings. She grew up in poor conditions and a bad household. They never had money, and her parents constantly fought. My maternal grandfather's alcoholism eventually caused diabetes and issues with his liver, which cost him both his legs and shortened his life. My mom's mother, my grandmother, died when I was about a year old. I don't remember her, but my mom said she loved me.

My two uncles, her younger brothers, can't read or write to this day. My mother dropped out of school in the ninth grade. She loved her father. She always spoke of him lovingly. She looked past his abuse because he was her father. Judging by her choices, she was filling a gap he left.

My father abused her physically, emotionally, and psychologically. But after breaking up, she quickly met another man, and they started dating. This was an upgrade in many ways.

For my father to enjoy inflicting pain, he had to have a victim. Mom proved to be a great target. She had low self-esteem, lacked any direction in life and had a knack for doing what she was told. It was a perfect fit.

Compared to my father, my stepdad Bret was a good guy. He didn't beat my mother. He never laid a hand on her. He helped me in ways my father never did. He taught me how to throw a football, a perfect spiral. He taught me how to shoot a basketball and how to start a fire as well as how to perfectly barbeque chicken. I remember the day we walked to the trailer park's park, where I shot and made my first basket.

While we had our differences, and I was not the easiest stepson to deal with, he was there when I graduated high school, and he was there when I got my heart broken for the first time. For a long time, I was angry my father didn't love me and angry at Bret for not being my real father. I probably messed up any chance we had at having a real relationship early on. Until I was about 16, I mercilessly reminded him he wasn't my real father, that I didn't have to listen to him – the normal stuff angry kids say to stepparents.

It wasn't until I was older that I realized all he had done for me, before our relationship soured. The positives he brought to my life, and they can't be overstated, were eventually overtaken by his alcoholism and jealousy. He put a wedge between my mother and us kids as he controlled access between us later when I was a teenager.

One thing he did was place a lock on his bedroom door, so we had to knock and ask permission to speak to my mother. Oftentimes we were told no or that we should "come back later."

Some people can be mean drunks. They hit walls or fight people. Bret wasn't like that. He always reminisced about times past and he'd cry a lot when he was drunk. Sometimes he'd talk to us kids about how much he loved us and things he regretted.

"I'm sorry I'm not your real father," Bret said. "I wish things were different ... that I could be a different man."

I remember he was always nicest when he wasn't sober. He's the only person I've dealt with directly I can say that about. Substances tend to wipe away inhibitions and show you the broken-down person – who they really are. He was no different. I recall many times, when I saw him come home from the store with a 24-pack of beer, I'd think to myself, "Yes! We get good Bret tonight." Worst-case scenario, he'd blast Kid Rock and make homemade tacos. That's a worst-case scenario I could happily get behind.

Mom and Bret were into having a good time, and drugs and alcohol were never too far away. Bret was the drinker; mom smoked weed. But they both dabbled in the other from time to time. I grew up watching her using marijuana daily. I graduated from high school in 2004. The day before graduation, she called me into her room and closed the door behind her. She was watching a televangelist on TV and she peered out the curtains to see if anyone outside was watching. After easing her paranoia, she sat down on the bed and looked over at me sheepishly, motioning me over to her. She handed me a pipe filled with marijuana with a sense of childish glee. Then she said:

"Hit this!"

To her, this was a big rite of passage. I demurred.

"You've got to be shittin' me," I thought. This was my graduation present from her: an opportunity to get high.

I used marijuana a handful of times as a kid. It was usually with an older friend or cousins of mine. In fifth grade a neighborhood friend Ryan who lived next to our studio apartment in North Omaha smoked with me. He was a freshman at Central High School. I wanted to be the cool kid. We hung out, watched *The Simpson's* and *Billy Madison* and played catch. We went to his garage and smoked pot out of a pop can. Some people say they don't get high the first time. Well, let me tell you, I did. High as a kite on a windy day.

In the summer of 2000, I walked the streets of Florence in North Omaha with my two older cousins Duane and Marcus, and we smoked a blunt. I was 14 and they were 17 and 21. I remember coming back to my grandparent's house, clearly high, eating a bunch of food, playing *WrestleMania 2000* on my cousin's Nintendo 64 and crashing like a log on the living room couch.

In 10th grade, I went bowling with a pair of friends in their early twenties. We smoked two joints in the back of their car, listening to Def Leppard's "Rocket." I could hear every drumbeat, every strum of the guitar. I understood clearly why Steve Clark, Def Leppard's guitarist, hit every note the way he did on the solo.

I knew weed wasn't a terrible drug; it wasn't like alcohol. But I saw early on what habitual use could do to some people. So, I actively dodged drugs and alcohol in my formative years, with the exceptions of those three times. I saw how it affected my mother and wanted no part of that lifestyle.

***

Mom loved me, I never doubted that. She just let her laziness seep into every part of her life. She never had a bank account or filed her taxes. This was because of student loans she took out when she was young that she never repaid and she blew the money. More than anything else, she never showed us kids the importance of bettering yourself. Whatever we accomplished through education, climbing the professional ladder, or by saving money – we didn't learn that from her. Her life lessons were quite literally: find a place to get comfortable, stunt your growth, and blame everyone else for your problems.

She had what psychologists call an external locus of control, the idea that all outcomes are the fault of others instead of yourself. This was lived out through actions and words. She had a deep mistrust of strangers, authority figures (bosses and politicians) and centers of power (churches and the state).

After leaving the trailer, Bret and Mom lived in a small apartment in North Omaha. He brought mom, my sisters and me to meet his mother and father one day. His mother was ailing from throat cancer and used one of those talk boxes to communicate. After the weirdness of that wore off, I grew to really like her in the short time we had. I have a picture from one of the visits. My Mom, Bret, and my sisters are in front. I was standing next to Bret hugging him. I looked goofy wearing his Chiefs hat backwards. He was a Chiefs fan, so I was too. Both of us had smiles ear-to-ear. Bret would never have kids of his own, so in many ways, this was his showing off "his kids," to his parents.

Back at dad's trailer, Eddie had moved out. I'm guessing my dad kicked him out, as Eddie didn't voluntarily leave anywhere. Filling the void in my father's life first was a woman named Lori. She was a heavyset blonde woman, with a raspy voice. Lori smoked a lot of cigarettes. She and my dad used to date, in the early 80s. She moved in only briefly, and it wasn't a serious relationship. Any woman with an ounce of sense knew to keep my father at arm's length. They knew what he was and wasn't capable of. I have no proof, obviously, but Eddie said she was a witch. Take that with a grain of salt. He wouldn't let me listen to Fleetwood Mac because he said Stevie Nicks was a witch, too.

Then something even more life-changing happened. My dad sat me down in the trailer and told me bluntly that there was a secret he had been keeping from me for a long time.

"You've got a brother," he said flatly.

"Mom is pregnant?" I responded.

"No, I had a son before I met your mom," he said. "He has a different mom than you do."

My head was spinning.

"What does that mean, daddy?" I asked.

"It means you've got an older half-brother," he said. "He's a year older than you."

"Do I get to meet him?" I asked.

"Yes, you do, son. He's moving in."

My head spun even more.

Whoa. I had an older half-brother. Dad wasn't lying. He was moving in. His name was Shaun. At age seven, I realized that life can change fast. In the past six months, dad and mom split up, we had a revolving door of roommates and then I found out I had a brother. It was exciting. What my dad didn't share with me was that my brother, his mom and her two daughters, of no relation to me, were also moving into our trailer.

Their mom's name was Anabelle. She was a shoot-from-the-hip, tell-it-like-it-is type of person. She didn't hide her dislike of things, issues or people. She and my father dated briefly, but her mother hated my father. So, after she got pregnant, back in 1984, her mom made her stop talking to my dad. I wouldn't have been here had it not been for that decision.

My dad's absence had a detrimental impact on my brother Shaun early on. He was a troublemaker like me. I sought my dad's attention and he sought my dad's presence.

Word had it, after Shaun was born in 1985, Annabelle left my dad and moved to Colorado. In the time she was gone, she had two other children with two other men. For as weird it was to have these new people in my life, I gained a brother. So I was content.

Her type of discipline was a bit different from my father's. My dad allowed her to punish all of us kids, my sisters included. This included pouring liquid soap in our mouths and making us hold it in there for 20 minutes. I remember her slapping me in the back of the head when she saw me spitting the soap on the ground when I thought she wasn't looking.

One time all of us kids had been cussing and fighting. Anabelle lined us up outside of a bedroom in the trailer, we stood in a single file line. One-by-one she brought each of us in there and closed the door.

WAP! WAP! WAP!

I could hear Shaun crying and begging her to stop. His high-pitched screams shuddered up my spine. I couldn't see Shaun being hit, but I felt it. Annabelle was hitting Shaun all over his backside with a belt. The swinging of the belt could be heard through the door by the clanging of the buckle on his back. It was more terrifying with this all happening behind a closed door. Then it was Shaun's middle sister Beckie's turn. Annabelle's strikes were staggered with the words to yelled.

"You…need…to….listen…to…what…I…say…do…you…understand?" She said between swings of the belt.

I knew I was next. My sister and I also got our turn with the belt. My youngest sister and Shaun's youngest sister were too small to get the belt treatment. I'm not sure what arbitrary rule or marker parents have for when it comes to a child being "old enough" to get the belt treatment.

Anabelle seemed to relish in handing out these beatings. It gave her power over us. Many people who have no control over their own lives want to exercise it somewhere else, even if it's a minute amount over small children.

She also made us stand in the push up position, with our hands on the ground, body flat and toes holding us up. We had to do this for 20 minutes at a time. I remember one time Shaun and I had fought with his sister. But instead of beating us with a belt, Annabelle made us stand that way. Shaun always "back talked" his mother when this happened, telling her how much he hated her for making him do this. He was used to this treatment by now, but still hated every minute of it. I did too. It was hell. I'd rather have the beatings. If we put our heads on the ground, giving us a little more support, she'd reset the timer.

I hated my dad for allowing her to punish us. She wasn't my mother. Bret, my stepdad, never punished us like this. I shouldn't have expected anything different from my dad though.

She and my dad didn't stay together very long. Dad and Lori were together for a few months, and Shaun came into our lives with his mom and sisters for half a year in 1993. As quickly as they came into our lives, they left. There was no story, no inside information, just an empty trailer. This left a big hole in my life. I had a best friend, a brother, and then Shaun was gone.

In that short time, Shaun and I grew close. Sure, we were young, but our classes at Pinewood Elementary in Omaha were just a few feet apart and we always clowned around together. I have a video my

22

grandfather recorded, a family video. Grandpa was known to pull out the camcorder to record gatherings and grab as much of our lives on film as he could.

There is a small clip of Shaun and me at my grandpa's house in March of 1993. We were both wearing wind breakers and hats to keep our heads warm on an early spring day when the snow was still thawing. Early spring birds chirped in the tall trees where my grandparents lived. Shaun and I had no idea grandpa was recording us. We were on the swing set in my grandpa's side yard, both swinging as high as we could go. You could hear us saying random gibberish to each other, Shaun saying it and me repeating it. The noises of the swing set and our yelling were only drowned out by the sounds of our laughter. Two kids being kids.

I've seen this clip maybe 20 times and it never fails to take me back to that moment, remind me of a positive time as a child. It also makes me think of my grandpa and Shaun. Planned or not, it makes me think of grandpa's ability to know this was a special moment – two brothers just getting to know each other. I'll always cherish this memory.

Chapter 5 – Fostered

In November of 1993, I was in second grade at Pinewood Elementary in Omaha. A group of young adults visited our classroom. They called themselves "Kid Ability." They were part of a nonprofit educating kids on what "good hugs" and "good touching" were, along with what "bad hugs" and "bad touching" could be.

The five adults in the group, all in the same blue shirt with a red "Kid Ability" logo, broke the class of about 25 students into small groups. In my group of four students, the man asked us a specific question.

"Do you kids know about a good hug and a bad hug?"

"Yes!" I said. Mom had the talk with me about what bad hugs and bad touching were.

"Good," he answered. "Has anyone else touched you in a bad way?"

"No, not bad hugs," I said.

"Okay. Good. What about spanking? Do your parents spank you?"

I was puzzled. I thought all parents treated their kids the way I had been treated.
Spanking? That was second nature. I got that anytime I crossed my eyes, it seemed.

"Yes," I said flatly.

"Oh," the man said. "Does it hurt? How much does it happen?"

"Yes, it hurts," I said thinking about how to respond to the next question.

I wasn't a liar. I told the truth.

"It happens all the time, anytime I get in trouble," I said after thinking about it.

"All the time?" the man said, looking up at another member of the Kid Ability staff.

I went on. I told them about when my dad punched me in the mouth and knocked my tooth out for playing with friends two blocks over without telling my parents where I was. The man didn't respond. By now another man with the group had come over and started taking notes on a small pad.

"Once when I was asleep, dad woke me up in the middle of the night by grabbing my leg and holding me in the air. Then he spanked me hard with a belt all over my body," I said to the man.

By then the man was furiously taking notes as the other knelt down and grabbed my shoulder.

"It's going to be okay, Brandon," he said. "I'm glad you told us. It's always good to tell the truth."

The man stood up and walked over with the other person who was taking notes. They chatted for a few moments. I could tell something wasn't right. They spoke with the other adults and with my teacher. The next thing I knew, they took me to the principal's office with my sister Brittney. Then the police showed up. They took us to a big gray building where my sister and I sat in a detective's office telling a large group of police officer's about my father's abuse.

"Hey son, do you want something to eat?" the detective said. "Are you hungry?"

"Yeah!" I replied.

"Me too! I'm hungry," my sister said.

"Alright come with me. Let's get you some goodies," the detective said.

He led us to a breakroom where a group of four officers sat and stood around a plain table, chatting, seemingly on break.

"Here, let's see what we got..." the detective said.

"Are those guys cops too?" I asked the detective.

"Yes, son. We are all cops here," he responded.

"Can I be a cop too?" I asked.

"Sure, son, today you're an honorary police officer," he said patting me on the back with a smile.

"Now what do you want to eat, son?" He pointed in the vending machine. "We got Zingers...Twinkies...mini donuts...crackers..." I interrupted him.

"I want the Zingers!" I said. My sister responded right after I did.

"I want chocolate donuts! Can I have milk too?" she said.

"Sure, let's see what we have here." He walked over to the breakroom fridge, which was covered in Husker football news clippings and magnet schedules. I was struck by the fact they had 1993, 1992, 1991 and 1990 Husker schedules. "It looks like we do have some milk. Do you want some too son?" he asked me, placing a carton of milk on the counter.

"No, I want water." I was never a fan of snacks with milk, I always wanted water with mine.

"Okay," he said, placing coins in the machine.

As soon as the Zingers hit the bottom of the machine, I pushed in the door and grabbed them, crinkling the wrapper. After the detective got the donuts, he led us out of the breakroom.

"Come with me, kids."

I learned, in time, that when cops offer you food it's usually a bad sign. But in the moment, I felt oddly valued, like I was a normal kid. Interesting it took being in the middle of a detective's office to feel that way.

By the time we got back to the office with a big long desk and no windows, there were a few more detectives there. The kind of guys you'd see in the movies, wearing slacks and dress shirts with a holster and gun.

"Have a seat, you two," an officer with a goatee said.

My sister and I sat down and the officer who got us snacks opened our Zingers and donuts, sat us down, and pushed our chairs in. My feet dangled back and forth, not touching the ground.

"We're going to record you when you talk to us, but don't you worry about the microphone and recording device," the goateed detective said.

They asked us a bunch of questions: What was it like living with mom and dad? Were they both mean? How about each of them on their own? How often did dad hit us? And mom? Did dad hit mom in front of us? Did they feed us? What were timeouts like?

They were hunting for answers and a reason behind the physical, emotional, and psychological abuses while getting a better understanding of a life lived with my father.

We went on and on for hours it seemed. They took copious notes. When we wrapped up, the officers led us through a corridor lit with flickering fluorescent lights. Then one of them opened a heavy door and the sun shined through as we walked out. The hefty door slammed hard behind us, signifying a portion of our normal life closing.

After getting my sister and me into the back of the police car, the two detectives drove to my grandmother's house. We lived in the trailer, but my youngest sister was at my grandma's. Perhaps that was the proxy site where they had my sister. I vividly remember seeing grandma hand off my sister, who was only three at the time, to a police officer. She then waved at us and blew kisses, just like she always used to do when saying goodbye. I know she was hurting. She was strong and she knew we were the ones who were going to be in pain, being ripped from the only family we knew.

***

My sisters and I slept somewhere new that night – a foster home. This house was much nicer than we were used to, but it was foreign. At first, I didn't know what to think. Our foster mom, Pat, allowed us a grace period to let us acclimate. But it was very different from what we were used to.

27

First, we ate three meals as a family. This was new to us compared to mom and dad's. We brushed our teeth before bed. That was new too. We went to church on Sundays. This was very new, and hard to get used to.

I thought I was a tough cookie. But deep down I was a softie. I just wanted hugs and to be loved. But I knew how to get attention in the end, even if it was negative attention. So, I acted out a lot. I cussed at Pat. I hit her. I hit the other kids.

Pat was in her late fifties. She was divorced, with six biological kids of her own, two sons and four daughters. There were two other foster kids at Pat's. I was the oldest kid in the house. It didn't take me long to figure it out and to take advantage of the circumstances. I was in a place where I wouldn't get beaten, swore at or belittled. Nothing they could do was going to top, for lack of a better term, what dad had done to me. I acted out in all ways imaginable.

Pat tried her hardest to show us love and affection and, even though I was a little bastard terrorizing her household, I took advantage of all the hugs and nurturing I could get. There was no shortage of them. She was easily the most selfless person I've met. We went to the park, the zoo, and we went to Adventureland as a family. I had the biggest party of my life for my eighth birthday in 1994, which was held at the Discovery Zone in Omaha.

Pat signed me up for youth baseball that spring. I was terrible. I played left field for the green Benson little league team. Any baseball fan will tell you where they put the terrible kids: in the outfield. I remember taking a line drive, throwing it into the stands behind home plate and hearing our mustached coach yelling.

"What are you doing, son?"

I couldn't hit a ball to save my life – but I had more fun than I ever had before. The most important people in my life, my grandparents, didn't miss any of the action. They attended every time I played. I loved seeing them, even though I was garbage on the diamond. My father, however, never showed up to one game – a fact my foster mom, Pat, reminds me of to this day.

After all that, I wanted attention. And I was starving for it. So, I acted out in class and got into a bunch of trouble there and back at the foster home. I bullied kids, I hit them, pushed them down, and laughed at them when they cried.

I got a kick out of them being hurt, much like my dad did. I got the attention I was starving for and none of the negatives that my dad brought. It was great, or so I thought.

One day, a kid and I argued in class and when we got to the bathroom during our break (we took class wide bathroom breaks back then), we fought. I punched him in the mouth, and he cried. I saw his sadness and reached out my hand, saying:

"It's alright Franky, let's be friends. Let's not fight."

He put his hand out to shake mine and I punched him square in the mouth.

"Take that, you little bitch!" I said laughing.

I thought I was a little badass. It got worse. My teacher requested I change classes because she caught wind of me abusing fellow students. Eventually I had to change foster homes too. I was acting out too much, fighting my foster mom and brother. My biological sisters stayed at the first foster home. I remember the day I left, I felt so sad. I wanted to cry out, please don't make me go! I love it here. I wanted to scream it from the rooftops. But I didn't, not that it would've worked. The damage was done.

I thought I was broken. How could I mess up this golden opportunity? The cops saw I was in a bad home, I thought, and they gave me a new one and I messed it up. I was just as bad as dad.

I still keep in contact with my foster mom. Back then I didn't understand her role in my life. Now, I see the support she offered when I had none. I wasn't used to it. I didn't know what to think then. Today, I call her mom.

At the second foster home, things were different. I felt it straight away. I was the youngest child. There were five other kids, ages 17, 14, 12, 10 and 9. The foster mom counted on the older kids to keep me in line. Much like a drill sergeant with their recruits. It didn't mean I straightened up. It just meant that no one was going to put up with me causing trouble. My second foster mother offered a strict household, something I needed at age eight. I only stayed with the second family for about six months. Some of the kids there were severally abused in their biological homes, just like me.

The foster brother I shared a room with was a ten-year-old Hispanic boy from Pueblo, Colorado. He had a rough upbringing; his dad was an alcoholic who beat on his sister and his mom.

One day after school, he went home to find his mom had left, never to return. It had a deep effect on him. He cried himself to sleep every night. I used to act like I didn't hear the whimpers because I didn't want to make him feel like he was soft. As a foster care kid, being hardened is a part of who you are – it's also the armor we wear to protect ourselves. It shows the world what we went through. He and I weren't close, but his story had an impact on me.

My mother finally got custody of me from the State of Nebraska, in fall of 1994. My sisters were still in foster care at the first home. Mom was living on the back porch of my uncle's apartment in North Omaha. We stayed there until mom got a place to live.

The porch wasn't heated and there was a gaping hole in the floorboards where rats, as big as your feet, lived. You could hear them rolling around and squeaking down there sometimes. I always told her when I heard them.

"Mom, do you hear the rats? They're moving around again," I said.

"Shut up, everyone has rats!"

"Grandma's house doesn't have rats!"

"Yes, she does. Everyone does. It's normal."

My mother was ashamed of how she lived, but instead of changing the situation, she wanted to change my mind, my perception of the world. Everyone was as bad as she was. This was "normal." At least on the back porch the cold mostly kept out the roaches who lived inside the house.

It had been nearly a year since I had lived with my dad in the trailer. On a cold night, I fell asleep watching my breath cloud the air. Thinking back over the previous year, it seemed like an eternity. From age seven to eight, I grew up so much. I knew this was another change for me. This would be the start of a new chapter of my young life.

Chapter 6 – Back To Normal

Mom and I finally moved out of the back porch of my uncle's apartment. We entered a program for single mothers at the Salvation Army with the help of the State of Nebraska. It gave us a place to live while mom searched for work. It was a two-part process. The first stage was a stepping-stone to the second part of the program. We stayed in a shared living situation. It used to be an office of some sort with three rooms and a bathroom. Two rooms served as sleeping quarters. These were huge rooms with ten beds apiece. Other families stayed in there with us. There was also a dining area and a shared area to watch TV.

We ate a lot of vending machine junk, because we didn't have our own food or a place to cook. I used to get skittles just to bite them open and drop them into my Sprite so I could watch the soda bubble up and change colors. I felt weird living with the other families. One single mother had short black hair and a newborn baby. She didn't know the father. Being innocent, and lacking social manners, I asked, "Where's the baby's dad?"

"I don't know," she responded without a second thought. "I don't know who the father is."

This blew my mind. I knew how babies were made. How could someone not know the father of their child?

Over the next month, my mother also got custody of my two sisters. After this, we were integrated into the full program. We got a two-bedroom apartment on the 5th floor of the Salvation Army.

It was much nicer than anything I'd ever lived in. It looked like a swanky 90s apartment like on the show *Friends*, with spacious bedrooms and bathrooms. I got my own room and even had my own bathroom with a new stand in shower.

It wasn't my mother's fault we went into foster care the first time. She hadn't abused us – Dad had – though court records I have indicate she "hadn't stepped in to stop the father's abuse of the children."

She felt vindicated when she got custody of us. Mom reminded us often of what dad put her through.

"He told me many times that I wouldn't ever get you kids back. Well I did and you're mine now," she said.

Now, in a position of power, she was ready and willing to use us as ammunition against my father. He had to go through parental counseling, learning how to treat children, how to punish us in a constructive way, etc. He finally reached all benchmarks set by the judge and could visit us without supervision. The judge also approved him for two weekends a month of overnight visitation. Before this we were allowed 90 minutes a week, supervised, to spend time with him.

In the Salvation Army, we had regimentation and a curfew. We lived very close to school, Walnut Hill Elementary, so getting there was never an issue. We got to eat cafeteria food, which to me was a plus because of all the different choices. Living on the 5th floor, we had a great view of 40th and Cuming streets in Omaha, overlooking Bemis Park. We used to beg mom all the time to take us to play on the playground.

I thought this was going to be the start for mom and dad, each on their own, to finally get it right. I was eight years old and I was able to be a kid.

Bret and mom were still dating, but he lived at his parents' house. He pushed mom, along with us kids, to move in with him. Bret, an Army reservist, happened to be nine years younger than my mother. Mom liked the idea of moving in with him, mostly because it would give her freedom from the state – no more curfews and she could smoke weed freely.

By the spring of 1995, we moved out of the Salvation Army. Bret's dad, Floyd, served in the Korean War. He was an old man, who drank a lot. As he drank, he became violent – the opposite of Bret's drinking. Oftentimes, Floyd would lash out at my mother. Once, during an argument, he threatened to shoot her. He even brought a gun out to show he wasn't joking, wildly waving it around. We ended up staying there for nearly a year. The only positive of living at Floyd's house was the puppy we got, a black lab named Balou.

***

33

In early 1996, my mom, Bret, my sisters, Balou and I moved out of Bret's dad's house and into a studio apartment in North Omaha. This place had about 450 square feet, and that is being generous. It included a small room, half of it converted into a kitchen nook, with a half bathroom. There was no central air in those old buildings and during the summertime we didn't have an air conditioning unit. There were three other apartments in the building. It just so happened to be where my mom lived on my uncle's back porch. This place was a hell hole. There were roaches and rats everywhere.

We had a pull-out couch that Bret and mom slept on. My sister Brittney slept on a broken-down love seat Bret found near the dumpster out back and my other sister slept on a chair. I slept on the ground with Balou and the roaches. I would wake up to them in my hair, crawling on my back or feet. Once I woke up with a dead roach stuck to my face. I didn't notice until I got on the school bus. Kids being kids, the others made fun of me for being poor and having roaches on my face. Several times I'd find roaches crawling in my backpack at school. There was no worse feeling of dread than that.

I hated the place. My dog Balou was about one year old at the time. He grew to be a big dog, about 110 lbs. We were already best buds. Living in this small space, we grew to be even closer. I always saw him as *my* dog and after that, the family did too. He showed me the most affection and wouldn't leave my side. We were inseparable. I used to talk to him at night when everyone had fallen asleep. He'd lick my nose and nuzzle my chest. It was all I needed. He had no idea what he meant to me in that hell hole. He was my support in those moments of need. He softened the blows and shielded me from the misery of living with my mother.

Mom's poor parenting affected Balou's life too. I had to hold him down the time we gave him home surgery after he ran away and got into a fight with an alley dog. We sewed up his ripped ear. There was no pain medication and we used regular sewing thread. He shook from pain and cried like a baby. I kissed his face, telling him everything was going to be okay. Later, when he suffered from terrible cysts on his body, including one which connected to his tail and wrapped around his spine, mom refused to take him to a veterinarian. Mom hated taking us kids to the hospital or the dentist, even though we had Medicaid, and Balou was treated the same.

Two of the four apartments in our building were usually vacant. The other occupied apartment belonged to my mom's brother. This was the same uncle who years earlier tried to get my mom to give him money for weed. His habits hadn't changed. Often, we'd go down to their apartment to "hang out." We'd watch TV, because we didn't have one. It was either Jon Claude van Damme movies, *Star Trek: The Next Generation* or *The X-Files*.

"Hanging out" literally meant the adults – my mom and Bret, my uncle and his wife – sat in the kitchen, smoked weed, read the Bible and talked about the end of the world on the other side of a blanket which was hung like a curtain separating the room with adults with the children's room. Most times, because we were so young, they made us come with them and sit in the living room of Barry's apartment, while they sat in the next room smoking and debating.

"Here hit this shit!" my uncle said between coughs after inhaling the smoke.

Barry's apartment was dark and dank. He covered all the windows with blankets. Some were Harley Davison, one was an eagle. You couldn't tell if it was night or day unless you looked at the front door, where you could see light peeking through the peephole. It smelled like old socks and dirty feet.

Barry's wife, Katie, was coincidently my stepdad Bret's sister. She had a kid from another man. His name was Jake. He was about five-years-old at the time and was mentally handicapped. He spoke with a speech impediment and would zone off sometimes.

Barry bullied Jake constantly. He made fun of how he spoke. He called him names and made him cry. It was a lot like how my dad treated me.

Jake could memorize movie quotes. He knew all the dialogue from *The Lion King*, back to front. He was also the best kid I've seen at *Donkey Kong Country* on Super Nintendo. Barry pawned Jake's Super Nintendo

35

when he needed a quick buck. This happened often. But he'd tell Jake that it was because he was being a bad kid. If Barry didn't have a real reason, he'd find or goad one out.

In 1996, Barry and Katie had a son named Nick. Jake and Nick were half-brothers, but they became fast friends. Barry, often high, would run around picking on all of us kids. My sisters and I remember he'd come up to us and open his arm pit. He called it "the Pit." The shtick went like this:

"Watch out now, it's the Pit!" Barry'd say, coming closer to us.

He'd open his arm, get close to us and wrap his under arm around our face. It was sweaty and stinky; I can smell and taste it now. Even after he let go and we wiped our faces, we smelled like dirty, putrid man sweat.

Barry often beat his own children and made them watch him have sex with their mom. I know because they both, aged six and three, at the time, told my sisters and me about it. Barry also liked to scheme the system, by driving around looking for "old ladies" to get in a wreck with so he could take them to court to get some cash.

"You guys have no idea. There's an untapped market of old ladies out here up to their necks in their dead husband's money and Social Security checks, just looking to get thrashed," he said.

Once at a Denny's he unscrewed an overhead lamp that was sitting above his table. A few minutes later as the waiter was taking his order, the lamp fell from its holder and struck him in the head, cutting him open. He took the owner to court and settled for a small amount of money – less than $2000 – but it was worth the squeeze.

My other uncle, Ernie, was my mom's youngest brother. He had a job as a "Ding Ding man," driving the ice cream truck around neighborhoods and selling ice cream. The thing was, he also illegally bartered ice cream to families for food stamps. This is the same uncle, who a few years later, took me with him on his job as a tow-truck driver. One night, after midnight, we were in midtown Omaha. Uncle Ernie looked over to me and said:

"Hey what do you say, we go pick up a couple hookers and have them give us some blow-jobs?"

I laughed. That's what you do when your uncle says stuff like that to you when you're 14. But then we drove down Leavenworth Street in Omaha actively looking for women to pick up. Luckily, he got a call from dispatch to pick up a vehicle near Benson, so we left. I'd come to find out later he was a meth head. He also made me watch porn with him in his bedroom with the door shut. He fast forwarded to the "good parts," Ernie's favorite parts, looking at me for approval each time he did this.

"I've done this with Becky," he said talking about his longtime girlfriend and mother of his children, essentially my aunt.

After about ten minutes of watching, Ernie left the room and told me to "get comfortable," pointing to a bottle of lotion and handing me the VCR remote. I waited a few minutes before leaving the room – I was unsure if he'd get mad for me not "doing" what he wanted. I felt dirty and used. I just can't quite describe the feeling I had then or even now. I told my mom and she yelled at him. Nothing more came from it. I haven't spoken to, or seen, Uncle Ernie since.

***

I think about my favorite memory from the studio apartment often. It was toward the end of the month and we were very low on food. We had a little bit of butter and less than 1/6th of a loaf of bread left. The refrigerator was a sad place where the butter sat alone with an open container of baking soda. Bret had my sisters and I check the couch for change. We scoured the whole couch, underneath it, between cushions, in the cracks – anywhere a coin could fall. We found three quarters and a handful of pennies, along with a bunch of lint and crumbs. My mom got home from work and we asked if she had any money.

"No, I'm broke," she said.

We weren't sad. We were on a mission. We checked the whole apartment, the couch, in jars and cups, in the kitchen drawers. Brittney and I took mom's purse and we dumped it out. We found receipts, lipstick, eye shadow, empty books of food stamps, and a coin purse. We opened the coin purse and found less than a dollar. Then Brittney took the purse and put her hand inside, scrubbing the liner. Hand to God, she pulled out not one, but two single food stamps. I remember them clearly. They were folded, brown and beautiful! We had a total of $3.50 give or take a few cents in coins and the two food stamps. I've never been so happy to shop in my life.

We walked to Albertson's which was only about ten minutes away. We walked into the air-conditioned grocery store – reason enough to make the walk on a hot summer's day – and went straight for the Hostess cakes. Back then, you could get a 6-pack of HoHos 3-for-$1. We bought two packs of HoHos, two packs of hot dogs, two packs of buns and a 6-pack of ramen noodles. We walked back home, with hearts full because soon our tummies would be full too. That night we feasted like kings!

Chapter 7 – Jackpot

It was a dream come true. I felt like I had hit the jackpot. My mother had gotten fed up with me and my pushback. She tired of me constantly reminding her I didn't need her in my life. She gave up custody of me to my father. As I was swimming like Scrooge McDuck in my winnings, I felt bad for my sisters who didn't get to move with me to grandpa and grandma's house. They were stuck living with my mom and Bret. To make matters worse, mom, Bret, Barry and his wife, along with their two kids and my sisters all moved to a house off 29th and Cuming Streets in Omaha shortly after I left. They pooled resources to move into their own place. Of course, they all claimed to live in the house as single families, maxing out state help via SNAP benefits, or Food Stamps.

Feelings for my sisters aside, I finally distanced myself from my mom's family. Even though I had two weekends with them every month, it was still a breath of fresh air. At least my sisters didn't have to live with my dad, as he was loving rent free at his parents' house with me after ruining the trailer grandpa bought for him.

The saddest part of moving out of my mom's was that I'd have to say goodbye to my best friend and dog, Balou. We got Balou in the summer of 1995. Bret found him in an alley on a hot July day while working on a roofing job. He was just a puppy. He was panting hard. Bret brought him in the car and gave him some water to drink out of his hand. Luckily for me, he decided to bring him home. Balou was a great dog. He had a deep bark that scared people and a strong tail he would bang on tables and walls to get out attention when he was hungry. He would always play with me, with toys or with tennis balls. It was as if he sensed when I was down and needed a pick-me-up. Many nights I cried myself to sleep on the floor in the studio apartment, Balou right there with me.

Many years later, when I was 21, I visited my mom's new apartment. Balou was old and broken-down, lying on the couch. He heard my voice and jumped up, barely able to walk. His spine was curled upward and his hips were out of place from dysplasia. I could see his ribs. He didn't care, he wanted to see me. He was howling with cries as I bent down to give him love. I will always remember that visit. Mom told me he hadn't moved in days. I sat on the couch and rubbed his head and patted his belly. He fell asleep on me. I was nine again. He died two weeks later.

Back in 1997, moving to my grandparents' also meant another change of schools. I went to Dundee Elementary for part of fourth and all of fifth grade. Anyone familiar with Omaha, knows Dundee is an upper middle-class neighborhood. This, to me, felt like living in "rich town." All the white kids I went to school with were rich. That meant they had moms and dads who worked full-time jobs and loved them.

After moving in with dad, I went to Florence Elementary in North Omaha. It was my sixth school in seven years. I attended schools with high poverty rates all my childhood, so this wasn't a big change for me. Kids who grew up in situations like mine had a hard edge and a chip on their shoulders. Most of the kids at the schools I attended were a lot like me. That affected classrooms. We weren't the easiest kids to get along with. We caused trouble in class and didn't listen to the teachers.

The difference between Dundee and Florence was spelled out in my group of friends. At Dundee my friends went to summer camps, they belonged to the Girls and Boys Scouts, they played violins and went on family vacations. At Florence, my group of friends were three kids named Steve, Clinton and Tony. Steve sold me a $5 bag of weed. I bought it to be cool, and threw it away as soon as I left school. Clinton could've passed as Beavis from *Beavis and Butthead*, and Tony was Steve's lackey. Steve and Clinton grew up to do time in jail, Steve for drugs (believe it or not) and Clinton for breaking and entering. Not sure what happened to Tony. The kids from Dundee? Every kid I knew went to college, three out of state. The opportunities were different, and the expectations were too.

When I first moved into grandpa's house, I lived in the small side room he created in the finished attic. The attic was broken up into three rooms: an office, a bedroom and a living room. I set up my bedroom in the office space, with a sweet pullout bed, TV and radio. I had a working Magnavox computer with Windows 95.

Where dad immersed us in abuse, my grandparents showered us in love. In many ways, my grandparents knew what we were going through. It was their son, whom they knew better than anyone, who caused all this pain. They tried to make up for his lack of love by pouring love over us. Grandpa and I grew close during this time, watching old World War II movies or episodes of *Cheers* and *Frazier.* Some of my best memories were in sixth grade, getting ready for school. Before grandpa gave me a ride to school at 7:30, we would watch two back-to-back episodes of *The Munsters.* He would have a cup of steaming hot black coffee, a couple slices of buttered toast and read his morning newspaper. Of course, *The Munsters* being a 60s TV show, I'd have questions about some of the pop culture references. He was always generous and kind dealing with me. He helped let me understand it was okay to be inquisitive and interested in the world around you. My questions about an old TV show were just a great example of his feeding my interest.

All these years later, my childhood's best memories come from just being with him and grandma. Perhaps they were trying to make up for their mistakes when raising my father. They knew he wasn't a functioning adult any way you sliced it. So, they went overboard on their love and affection to us. They were the glue that held the broken pieces of me together.

Eventually, I moved from the attic with my grandpa to an extra bedroom on the second floor of the house. It was a small, dorm-like room which was perfect for me. I still had my TV, stereo, and a lock on the door. But ultimately dad took that out so he could spy on me. He didn't like me being in control, and the lock represented a small bit of power I had. He would come to my closed door and peek through the hole where the deadbolt used to sit. It creeped me out. Still, I was at home. Dad's abuse was mostly verbal and emotional during this time, making fun of how "fat, clumsy, and dumb" I was.

"All three traits you got from your goddamn mother – you didn't learn that shit from me."

Grandma and grandpa served as a barrier. They shielded me from dad both directly and indirectly. His abuse changed at grandpa's house.

During the summer of 1997, I became the butt of more jokes and ridicule, as my dad had someone new to get attention from, my cousin Duane, while I was sacrificed.

He even made new nicknames for me. He called me "Fatty McFatterson" and "The Burger Bandit" as well as "Chubs." Every time he'd call me these, Duane would burst out laughing and it would fuel my father more. Nothing makes a comedian feel wanted like a laughing audience.

"Brandon, get your fat ass down here – right fucking now," dad said, continuing the attacks.

"We're going to have to get you a sports bra, aren't we, Chubs?" he chipped back, seeing Duane was laughing for him.

It was like he was heating up, like Steph Curry does when shooting 3-pointers, or like Eddie Murphy did when he was onstage doing standup. That's the only way I can explain it. In that moment, he was a performer as much as he was an abuser.

I asked Duane recently what he thought of those times. He responded on Facebook chat:

"It was usually some sort of spin on whatever was 'trending' on TV or in print, etc. He'd replace it with the word "fat" or "round" or something similar. The nicknames would be really silly and nonsensical. He used to stop me midstride, midsentence, 'Like what did you just call him? Jesus. He's your son, for goodness sake.'"

I don't blame Duane for any of this, how could I? He was three years older than me, but after he turned 14, he didn't hang around us as much.

Chapter 8 – Night Stalker

Dad's abuse of the women he was with evolved after my mom. This was apparent with a new girlfriend dad met in 1994. After mom, dad dated Lori and Annabelle, both old flames dad had before he met my mother. The newest woman in my dad's life was Debra. She dated dad from 1994 to 1997. She was a smart woman who dealt with depression and self-image issues. Because of that, she was perfect for my father. She was divorced and had two kids, but she didn't have custody. When Debra and dad first got together, they lived in her apartment in Papillion. Back then, dad had a solid job at Plastilite, a company on the outskirts of North Omaha.

They decided to move to my grandpa's house to save money while Debra tried to get her kids back. Later in their relationship, he would make fun of Debra to Duane and I. Telling us of their sexual exploits in great detail. He called her "Debbie flaps," a reference to her genitalia. He also called her "flapjacks," because her breasts were "like pancakes," he said. It was like a game, with secret code words, and my cousin and I used to laugh when he said things like this. One side of me knew this was wrong then, but the other part of me was just happy it wasn't me who he was picking on now.

He never hit her that I know of. But he abused her emotionally and psychologically. Living with my father was not an easy thing to do. This took a toll on her and she grew apart from my father. She also started secretly dating a co-worker.

One day in late 1997, Debra decided to drop the bombshell on my father. She was dating someone else and she was leaving him. She already put a down payment on an apartment. My dad hit the wall. He wasn't going to be left behind.

"What the fuck do you mean – You're leaving me?" my father yelled at her.

"I'm simply telling you that this isn't working and hasn't worked for at least a year," she said, frustrated dad wasn't getting her point. "I'm done with this. I can't take it anymore and I want out. What don't you understand? Over the past three years, we've piled up thousands of dollars in credit card debt. You were never going to help me, were you?"

Dad always wanted to be in control. So, he reminded her of the mistakes she made with him.

"Haha, looky here, sweetheart, that debt is in your name not mine – got it?" he responded. "Looks like you played your cards the wrong way."

My father was not below being petty. A bully loves nothing more than to know he's gotten to you. That was all he needed to continue on. He knew he lost her, so he was going to wreak maximum damage.

They were in my dad's room on the second floor of the house. It was late fall and NFL football was on the TV. I could hear the announcer calling play-by-play between their bouts of yelling. Debra had brought home donuts from the grocery store and I was just finishing up my second one, sitting in the kitchen at the bottom of the stairs. It didn't hit me how much of a change this would have on my future in the moment. That day she left and never came back. My dad didn't like rejection.

She moved as far away from my dad as she could get without leaving town. One Friday, my dad picked my sisters up from my mom's house and brought them back to my grandpa's. My dad had a cut on his head.

"What happened to your head, dad?" I asked.

"I found out where Debra lives," he answered. "I went over there to talk to her and her boyfriend was there. We got into a fight and I beat his ass."

44

I believed him, but looking back, I'm not so sure. He told me he punched her boyfriend in the head a few times and during the fight he slipped down the stairs. Because he was wearing moccasins he slipped when he was pushed. He claimed he cut his head on the railing trying to catch himself. I thought this was the end of it. Boy, was I wrong.

***

That weekend I went to my mother's house for the bi-weekly visitation. It was a normal weekend by any standard. When dad picked me up, I could tell his mood was off. Something was amiss. Though he was an abusive, controlling, manipulative individual, he was always looking to get a laugh. While dad jokes and puns were wasted on him, he made up for it with dirty, in-the-gutter, low-brow wit. He made fun of heavyset women in public and he catcalled pedestrians as we drove past them. This day though, I got into the car and Dad didn't say much to me – he avoided small talk. This was always a bad sign.

We left from my mom's apartment in North Omaha, and instead of taking the 10-minute ride down to Highway 75 North to grandpa's house in Florence, we went to South Omaha. I knew right away something wasn't right. After a few minutes, it was obvious we weren't going to grandpa's.

"Where are we going?" I asked my dad after a few minutes.

"To the gas station," he said. "You want to get a Pepsi?"

"Sure!" I replied. I enjoyed Pepsi.

We continued our journey to the gas station, stopping at a BP in South Omaha. My dad was wearing his normal get up: black jeans, moccasins, a 1994 Huskers "Unfinished-Business" t-shirt, which was always tucked in to his jeans. His outfit was complete with a leather wallet

45

connected by a chain to his jeans belt-loop. We both bought 20-ounce bottles of Pepsi.

"That it sir?" the attendant asked my father.

"Yeah, that's it," my dad replied, handing over two single dollar bills and putting the handful of change he received from the cashier into his pocket. He nodded at the gas station attendant, said goodbye, and we left.

We drove around in circles for hours that night. Dad brought a bunch of CDs – Van Halen, Foreigner, Bad English, and Slaughter. He would wind himself up listening to songs about holding out hope in failed relationships. It seemed to keep him in that dark mindset, where he wanted to be.

Then, we drove around the same block three times. After a couple times around the place, I saw Debra's car parked in the back, so I put two and two together. We drove slowly, dad looking at her windows to see if her lights were on. We even went around to the alley and parked behind her garage where we wouldn't be seen to check the back lights. Then my dad said:

"Hey boy, go check her car. See if the doors are locked."

I paused. My dad was asking me to do something wrong, even illegal. I knew it then. But I listened. I got out of the car. He pulled ahead a few houses. I walked slowly to her car and pulled the handle. It was unlocked. I looked back to show him that it was open. He gave me a signal to keep looking. So I looked in the middle console, rifling through receipts, bills and a birthday card. I don't know what he was hunting for, maybe certain papers, notes, anything to fuel his jealous isolation. I closed the door softly and walked back to the car with the bills and receipts.

"What the fuck took you so long, boy? What did you find?" He ripped the stuff from my hands.

Then we circled around the building a few more times and he said,

"Go check her mailbox, see what's in it."

So I did. While I was opening the box, I was sure she was going to catch me. But nothing happened. I found a cable bill and water bill. He snatched those from me too, ripping them open, tossing the envelopes on the ground.

"She's hardly using any water. Where is she going for it!" My dad said exasperated, grasping at straws. "Go check her window. Be quiet when you walk up the stairs. Peek in without being seen. Let me know what you find."

I did walk up there slowly and peeked in. Her two sons were there, the youngest drawing in a coloring book, the eldest playing video games. She was cooking in the kitchen, making macaroni and cheese. She glanced up at me, and in a look of shock and bewilderment, did a double take. She ran to the door.

"What the hell are you doing, Brandon?"

I couldn't even muster a word in response.

"Did your dad put you up to this?" she asked.

I simply nodded.

"Please leave and don't do this again," she said. "I'm calling the cops."

The next day she filed a protection order on my father. That didn't stop him. We kept going back. This went on for months. I'd go along when he needed someone to help him which ended up being every night when it got dark. He made me go to her second-floor apartment, climbing the stairs slowly and quietly. Somedays we could see her looking out her window. Others all the lights were off. One night, I saw her through the glass. She was sleeping on the couch. She had fallen asleep while reading a book.

Then, one day, her car was gone and the lights were offs.

"Go in and check the windows, boy," my dad barked.

There was nothing in the apartment. She moved (on with her life).

***

Within months he was dating a new woman. We'll call her Zelda. Why Zelda? That was the nickname he gave her, behind her back, because she "looks like Zelda from Pet *Semetary*," he told me.

He and Zelda dated for a few months in early 1998. It was hot and heavy, but it wasn't too serious. She lived in Council Bluffs, while we still lived in North Omaha at my grandparent's house.   One night when she visited, he was already in a terrible mood. I'm not sure what was bothering him this night. My two sisters were there as it was dad's weekend for visits. My youngest sister started crying and called for dad. I heard the commotion and opened my door and saw dad run out of the room and fly down the stairs.

"What the fuck is going on," he barked at my sisters.

"Brittney bit me!" my youngest sister said.

Brittney, who was 10, started crying and choking. I was in my bedroom, but my door was open. I heard everything.

"Bite me, you stupid bitch! Bite me!" my dad screamed.

He had forced his hand inside her mouth and pulled her up the entire stair case by her jaw. He threw her on the ground at the top of the stairs and kicked her into her bedroom yelling:

"Don't you ever fucking bite her again, you dumb little cunt! DO YOU HEAR ME?"

I knew what happened was horrific and terrible. But I was a tough little kid, so I had to act tough. I laughed in front of a clearly distraught Zelda, who had also witnessed the entire episode from the doorway of my dad's bedroom. We locked eyes, me still laughing.

"That not funny one single bit, Brandon," she said to me.

I didn't even respond. I knew she was right but wanted to act like a hard ass, so I just continued laughing and closed my bedroom door. Shortly after that, their relationship got rockier. He started showing his true colors more – if that attack on Brittney wasn't enough for her. He started controlling Zelda. His bad temper, manipulation and pettiness were enough for her to run for the hills. I remember the night Monica Lewinski gave her interview to Barbara Walters because I was sitting in the living room of Zelda's apartment with her daughter, who was in her early twenties. We could hear my dad yelling and Zelda crying. Eventually, she opened the door yelling: "Get out, now!" It was an awkward exit. I didn't say goodbye to anyone. I just stood up and walked out with my dad.

We came back after midnight. My father and I left grandpa's house, went to the nearest gas station to fuel up and get Pepsi's. Then we headed off for a night of stalking his ex-girlfriends and listening to 80s hair metal. By then, I knew what we would be doing without my father saying a word. As we were leaving her place, when she kicked my dad out, I remember thinking, "Yeah we'll be back."

We arrived at her apartment. We parked and we sat there for hours. He noted when lights would turn on or off inside.

"Someone must be using the bathroom," he said. "Wonder if it's her?"

I fell asleep and he jarred me awake.

49

"Wake up, boy, stay with me," he said.

At this moment I realized I was filling a void in his life, even at a diminutive level. I was keeping him from being alone. I felt sad for him. I also wondered if we should leave and go home.

"How long are we staying tonight? Can we go home?" I asked.

"We'll go home when we're done. Sit back and shut up," he replied.

Often on these trips, I'd wake up when we'd arrive back at my grandparents' house. Some of these trips happened on a school night. My dad would tell me that I could skip school if I went with him. That was an easy sell by then. I was 12 and what 12-year-old didn't want to skip school?

The stalking of Zelda went on for several weeks. She finally went to court to file a protection order against my father. This was the second restraining order filed against him and it wouldn't be his last. We kept going over to Zelda's. Sometimes during the day we'd go to her job and check her car doors to see if they were open. Finally, one day she noticed we were outside. She came out and yelled.

"I've called the cops, you'd better get out of here," she said.

"I just want to talk, come down so we can talk," he answered.

"Why are you doing this to me? Think about what this is doing to your son," she said, now looking at me. "You just need to leave me alone so I can move on with my life. What don't you get?"

She was at her wit's end.

He wasn't strong, he was weak, and she was right. He had no control over his impulsive decisions or over his emotions. Finally, we left. A few days later, my dad showed up at her job, again, breaking the protection order. He would spend a week in jail later that summer for the violation. It wasn't the last time he would see a jail cell.

Chapter 9 – Taken Away

My cousin Duane described my father perfectly.

"He is criminalistic in all facets of his existence. It's always the thrill of getting over on someone. He ingratiated himself to those he perceived as a threat and stomped with shitty shoes anyone who displayed "weakness," by really caring for him and making the mistake of letting him know it."

My dad liked to gross me out. There were no limits. One time when he dropped my sisters and me off for a weekend at my mother's house he waited until after my sister's got out of the car and said to me:

"When you give your mom a kiss, just remember my dick has been in her mouth."

It disgusted me. I told him that. He laughed in my face, driving off. He loved saying stuff like that to me. The dirtier, the more I got grossed out, the better. He talked about having sex with my mom. What she liked in bed. When I got fed up, he'd slap me on the back, laughing, like he played a practical joke on me. It made me not like to be around my mom, even more than before. He brought up how she compared to other women he was with.

That wasn't the extent of it. He tried to embarrass us kids by walking around with his underwear pulled up the crack of his ass, as if he was walking around in a G-string. He did this often. He liked to come up to me, yelling:

"Hey son, do you want to see where you came from?"

Before getting a response, he'd pull his pants down and expose his genitals and wave them in my face. He did this to me, or at me, many times. I didn't know why. I felt dirty and used, like I didn't matter to him.

I remember when he did this in front of my half-brother Shaun for the first time. I was there.

"What the fuck, dad? What is wrong with you?" Shaun said.

That same year, a friend of my dad's came over to play *Goldeneye*, the James Bond game, on Nintendo 64 with us. It was a fun game, but we couldn't beat a few levels, like "The Cradle." Dad's friend was very good at playing video games. He was a good guy, one of the few actual good men my dad knew that still wanted anything to do with him. He went to church a lot and invited us, too, but we never went.

That night he played "The Cradle." My dad laid in his water bed under the covers. Gary was sitting on a folding chair in front of the bed, facing the TV. I turned around to see if dad had fallen asleep, as Gary was getting pretty far in the level, nearly to the part where we kept getting killed. Dad was fondling himself underneath the blankets. I looked over to him, noticing what he was doing. I shook my head at him, and grimaced.

I thought, "Since he saw me, he'll get embarrassed and stop." But instead of being embarrassed, he grabbed his erect penis and pulled the blanket away to show it to me. Even then, I knew this was wrong and I felt sick to my stomach. He laughed at me without making a sound or getting the attention of his friend. To him, this was a joke. But it wasn't a joke. Father's don't fondle themselves in front of their sons and they don't get excited when their sons are revolted by it.

He liked to run around, bend over and spread his ass cheeks in my direction, grabbing them like Jim carry did in the Ace Ventura movies. But unlike Jim Carrey, my dad wasn't wearing underwear. He exposed his anus to me. This repulsed me to no end. But, you could never show him you were bothered by it. That was capital. If you did, he knew you were grossed out and it gave him reason to do it again.

When I was about 10-years-old and he was living at grandpa's house, he called me into his room.

"Hey, boy, let me show you something," he said.

This was code that he meant he was planning on showing me something to gross me out. He turned on the TV and I saw two people having sex. It was a pornography film. The woman was heavyset and old. This was one of his fetishes, I'd come to find out.

53

"You see that?" he asked me. "The man is licking her clitoris. It's also called the 'man in the boat.' Women love it when you lick it. Your mom loved it when I licked hers."

"Dad stop saying that," I said.

"Oh, stop being a pussy. Sit down, watch this. It'll make you a man."

The man continued to perform cunnilingus on the woman. They changed positions with the man lying underneath her.

"You see this, watch it boy," my father said wanted me to see what was happening.

The woman came to climax, "squirting" on the man's face.

"Isn't that great? That's how you know you ate the biscuit good, son," he said enjoying his time teaching me the ins and outs of the female anatomy and sex acts I was too young to understand.

It felt gross. My stomach felt uneasy. But I wanted to make him happy and proud of me. So I kept watching.

"What are they doing now?" I asked my dad.

"He's gonna fuck her in the ass." My father was never one for words.

"Why is he going to do that?" I asked.

"Because it's tighter," he said. "Here, give me your hand."

He took my index and middle finger and wrapped his hand around them.

"This is what a pussy feels like," he said gripping my hand loosely. "It's nice, it feels good. But sometimes an ass feels better. Here, this is what an ass feels like."

His hand gripped my fingers tighter.

"Does that hurt your wiener?" I asked.

"No, don't be stupid," he said. "It feels good and it gives you power."

We continued watching the porn film until the end of the scene. He made me watch porn with him many times over the next few years. It made me a man. My father never touched me sexually and he never made me touch him. That makes me feel slightly better about the abuse,

54

as others have had it worse. Then again, that's just what mom and dad always told me. In some way it diminishes what he did.

My dad brainwashed me to believe it was my mother and her family that were trash. But he was a monster, a chameleon. He could blend in for long enough to get by, but his true colors always came through.

Chapter 10 – A Fateful Encounter

Grandma got sick in the spring of 1999 and dad finally started getting over his past relationships. Dad and I moved out of my grandparents' and into a subsidized apartment complex in South Omaha. I started at a new school. Things were finally starting to slow down. I was 13 and it was summertime. That meant less school and more time with dad, but he was finally coming out of his anxiety filled shell. We stopped going on the nightly rides and he finally stopped talking about Debra and Zelda.

I had a genuine hope that things were going to click for dad one day. Maybe this could be the start of his change. Perhaps he would see the light, understand his wrongs, and try to fix himself. He was grandpa's son, after all. The apple isn't supposed to fall that far from the tree, is it? I thought that summer: Maybe one day, dad will be a good father, like my friends' dads at school. Their dads took them fishing and taught them how to throw a football. Their dads believed in them.

An old friend of my father, named Tony, came back into his life that summer. They attended high school together at Tech High in Omaha in the late 1970s. He was a sleazy guy who started his own ministry program. Tony got an online certificate and became a pastor. He used it to trick people into giving him money, with the guise of bettering youths in the community. Specifically, Tony helped under-aged girls who came from broken homes. He helped house them, paid for their schooling and found them employment. This mostly meant tricking them, letting them live with him and giving them cash to do what he wanted.

I spoke with one of the girls, who was 14 at the time. She said Tony made her do sexual things with him and even sleep in his bed at night. She knew what she was getting herself into, she told me, but how can a 14-year-old consent to anything sexual with an adult three times her age?

Tony had a handful of girls he was "helping." Some came and went from his house as they pleased, others stuck around for his day-to-day abuse. My dad looked up to him. At least it seemed that way. My dad never took part in this "ring of abuse" that I know of, but he didn't steer clear of Tony when he found out. He put him down behind his back for being a child molester, all the while, letting me be alone with him.

Tony introduced dad to a woman named Kim. She was about 35-years-old and had three kids. She and my father hit it off that summer. Within days of meeting she was spending the night at my dad's apartment and we were staying at her house as well.

Their relationship had its first test within a week. The stalking of Debra and Zelda came back to bite him. Both women had filed protection orders against my father and he had broken both court orders. The judge sentenced my father to a week in jail. My father was in a bind. Having nowhere to turn in a tight spot, he asked his new girlfriend if she'd watch me for the week. It was June, so I was out of school. She said yes, and I stayed at her house.

I spent the time she was at work watching old VHS tapes of the *Star Wars* trilogy. The remastered re-release had dropped in 1999. I wasn't a huge fan, but I watched them all to pass the time. I also watched *Blade Runner, Men in Black, Total Recall* and about every Jean-Claude van Damme movie you could imagine, including *Double Impact*. I also played her old Super Nintendo. To this day, I hate being alone. I get bored easily. It wasn't mom's house, though, that's for sure. So at least there was more to do.

Dad didn't want mom to find out he was in jail for two reasons. First, he didn't want her to use this as fuel to get custody back. Second, he didn't want to seem weak to my mother.

My father called everyday he was in jail. I remember when I first spoke with him I told him:

"Watch out for Big Bubba!" a reference to a jail cell mate who was potentially going to take advantage of and sexually assault him.

Obviously, this was a terrible joke – but it was a chance to turn the tables on him, and he was in a place of weakness. He didn't like that one bit.

"Shut the fuck up, boy! That shit ain't funny. You wouldn't last a minute in here."

He wasn't wrong, but I wouldn't put myself in there, I thought.

Kim and I didn't grow closer, per se, as she was working long hours and we didn't know each other well. My dad and she had only dated for a few weeks. She would return late in the day with Burger King or Pizza Hut for dinner. She was a very nice lady though, warm and welcoming. When my dad got out of jail, he was back to his old self very quickly: no job and no prospects of one.

One day in July, just a few short weeks after he got out of jail, my father and I argued. I was pushing his buttons and he was biting right back. He started yelling at me for some toys I left on the ground at Kim's house.

"Go pick up that shit, boy," he said. "I'm not fucking around with you. Do as I say."

I was trying to explain that what was on the ground wasn't mine. Some were clothes that belonged to Kim.

"That isn't mine, it belongs to your fat bitch," I said, knowing exactly what I was saying.

While saying this, I knelt down to pick up the toys and clothes. I turned around to get his reaction. I heard two loud steps and felt a pop. Then everything went black. I woke up on the ground, my head throbbing,

58

and everything blurry. My sight slowly came into focus and I could see my dad sitting in a chair, shaking his head. He'd punched me in the nose and knocked me out. He showed zero remorse. In fact, he was proud of his work.

"Do you have anything else you want to say, boy?"

I shook my head, crying, covered in blood with my head pounding.

"Good. If you want another lesson, just say the fucking words."

He baptized me in my mother's blood with a head butt to her nose. Now I laid on the ground christened by my own bloodshed. The official sacrament of my father.

Kim was kneeling over me, wiping up the blood with a towel.

"It's going to be okay, honey, we'll get you cleaned up," she said.

She wiped me clean but I had a pounding headache. I was so angry with Dad, I called my mom.

"Mom!" I said through tears. "Dad punched me in the nose and knocked me out, I'm covered in blood!"

My father yelled in the background.

"Yeah, I punched him! I'll do it again. You think I'm afraid of the police? I'm not! Go ahead and call them. I'll kill him and cut him into a thousand pieces. You won't ever find him!"

He wanted her to hear every word. She did.

I had never heard my dad make a threat like that to me. I didn't know if he was calling her bluff or if he was serious. One thing I did know was he didn't care for me at all. I was just a pawn for him, just like everyone else in his life. I knew that now.

***

A few weeks passed. It was Monday, Aug. 16, 1999. My father had taken one of his patented late afternoon 4-hour naps. He woke up about 10 minutes before Kim got home from work. He walked out of the dark bedroom in a white t-shirt and gym shorts. He looked disheveled. His hair was a mess. The desk fan dad always used when he slept was still on. At about 5:30, Kim came home after working all day. She was clearly distraught. My father had just woken up from the nap, and he was never in the greatest mood for the first hour. This night was no different.

Kim went to her bedroom in the basement to change out of her work clothes. Meanwhile dad was sitting in the kitchen watching the news on a small TV. After a few minutes, she came back upstairs.

"Hey sweetie," she said to her young daughter. "Are you hungry?" The young girl nodded. "Let's get you some dinner."

She set her daughter and youngest son in the booster seat and highchair. She asked my dad why he hadn't started making dinner yet.

"Were you too busy?" she asked.

"Don't start with me, woman," he said.

Tick! Tick! Tick! Tick!

She started the stove up and pulled two pans out of the cabinet. On the menu tonight was canned corn and ravioli. She turned to my father to tell him what was on her mind. Her youngest son's father had called her earlier that day while she was at work.

"He doesn't want anything to do with our son!" she said, looking for encouragement. "What kind of father doesn't want anything to do with his son?!"

"Kim, dial it back," he said. "Calm the fuck down. You're getting all worked up for nothing. You can't make the guy do anything. All you're doing is getting upset, and I just fucking woke up, I don't want to hear this shit."

"Are you kidding me," she said exasperated. "I worked all day long and just had an argument with my son's father. It was a bad day for me, okay? I get home and want to share it with you and all you can do is tell me to shut the fuck up?! What did you do all day? Sleep? I know the answer to that question..."

"Bitch, don't fuck with me," he said through clenched teeth, pounding the table with his fist.

This scared her two youngest kids at the table.

"You don't want to see me angry," he warned her.

The tension in the kitchen got to be too much to handle. It reminded me of the night my mom chased my dad out of bed with a butcher knife.

"What, are you going to punch me in the nose, too?" she asked, stirring the ravioli.

Without another word, he got up out of the chair and picked up the pot with ravioli from the stove. He threw the cold contents, which hadn't warmed up yet, all over Kim's face and shirt. Then he slammed the pot on the ground. There was ravioli everywhere. Her eyes opened wide in disbelief. Her daughter started crying and so did her 18-month-old son. Kim had enough.

"That's it!" she screamed. "You're fucking out of here. I want you gone! NOW!"

My father walked over to the kitchen door to leave. But before he got there, he stopped and punched the drywall in the entryway three times, letting out aggravated roars to scare her and the kids. There were now two holes in the wall. Kim tried to chase him out of the kitchen.

"I'm going to get your shit. I want you the fuck out of here," she said. "Get out of my way!"

They shoved each other in the kitchen doorway. He pushed her into the cabinet near the entryway. Then he shoved her out of the way, grabbed a can of Pepsi from the dining room table, shook it up and opened it. He sprayed her face, and shook it all over her. There was Pepsi everywhere, all over the walls in the dining room, and all over their shirts.

Kim screamed louder.

"You son of a bitch! What are you doing?"

They reached the living room. The sound of fighting increased furiously. The ravioli was caked in her hair, and Pepsi was dripping everywhere. They continued shoving each other, fighting to be ahead of the other person. Now it was a fight to not be the last to get downstairs to get dad's things. Kim's oldest son, who was five, was in the living room watching cartoons on TV, waiting for dinner to be ready. I stood near him, after leaving the kitchen.

He was crying loudly.

"Why are you hurting my mommy!?" he screamed to my father, who didn't even hear him.

Dad was locked in tunnel vision, just like the day ten years earlier when he head-butted and broke my mother's nose. Kim and my dad were still yelling at each other by the time they hit the living-room.

"Stay up here and leave me alone. I'm getting your shit and you're leaving for good," she said.

They ran into the entrance of the house. My dad tried leveraging himself ahead of Kim at the top of the stairs that led to the basement. I wanted to get out of the way of my father. I knew what he was capable of. I stood in the living room at this point, watching in silence from a few feet away as he yelled at her.

"Fine! If you want to go down the stairs, you'll go down them...."

He extended both of his hands into the center of her back and shoved her as hard as could. She screamed, falling face-first down the stairs. There was a loud thud, and everything went silent.

Chapter 11 – To Tell The Truth

Kim went down the stairs headfirst. There were two loud thuds. Her head hit the low hanging ceiling on the steep staircase, snapping back. She plummeted to the ground. Almost instantly, my father ran downstairs.

I stood motionless, without saying a word. After a few moments, I ran to the top of the stairs.

"Kim, baby, wake up!" my dad said in a panic, rolling her over on her back. "Baby stay with me. I'm so sorry!"

My dad had run into the bedroom to get the cordless phone to call an ambulance. Kim was lying on the floor, motionless, her eyes wide open staring up the stairs, looking directly at me, as if she was screaming at me:

"Brandon, why didn't you stop him! If only you had spoken up, this wouldn't have happened."

That has haunted me for 20 years.

She didn't say a word. She was unconscious with her eyes open. A few moments later, my dad was on the phone with 911, standing next to her immobile body.

"Hello, yes, my girlfriend fell down the stairs and is unresponsive," my dad said frantically, lying to the dispatcher. "I don't know what happened. She was at the top of the stairs and she slipped and fell. There's a piece of metal that separates the linoleum in the entryway from the carpet on the stairs, I've been telling her to nail that down for weeks now..."

I couldn't believe what he was telling the dispatcher. I could hear all the cries now. Kim's daughter had gotten out of the booster seat and was in the living room crying with her older brother. My dad gave the dispatcher the address and hung up the phone. He came upstairs.

My father and I made eye contact as he paced in the living room. In a moment of raw emotion, we locked eyes and ran into each other's arms. We hugged and both started bawling. I'd only seen my father crying one other time in my life. This was completely different. He was crying like a child, we both were. It was as if he was crying out for someone to save him.

We weren't the only ones crying.

"What did you do to my mommy?" Kim's son cried at my dad.

"She fell, son, I didn't do anything," he lied. "You saw it, Brandon, didn't you?"

Spineless, I nodded in agreement. My dad started explaining to the kids what he had told the dispatcher.

"We're going to save your mom, son, she's going to be okay. I promise," my dad said, feigning empathy. In this moment, he was playing the part of the older brother who had hit his sister and was trying to explain to her that she wasn't hurt, so she wouldn't tattle on him, so he wouldn't get in trouble. But instead of being an adolescent, he was 37-years-old.

In the distance, we could hear the ambulance sirens growing louder, closer. Within a few minutes, the ambulance arrived with a fire truck. Paramedics in blue shirts came busting through the door with a stretcher. They didn't need to ask any questions. As soon as they opened the door, two of them looked directly downstairs and could see Kim lying there. They jumped down the stairs. The next thing I knew they had ripped her shirt off, perhaps looking for other injuries. But they brought her up on the stretcher, topless. As they took her out the front door, they used equipment to help her breathe. Outside, about eight neighbors on

65

the block stood gawking at what was unfolding. Even then, I wanted to yell at them to all go inside – to stop looking at her. But who was I to say anything? I lied to protect my father.

As the paramedics sped off, two police officers pulled up, parked, and walked inside. They separated me and my dad from the kids. They questioned us all. My father and I kept up the lie about the break in the metal between the carpet and linoleum. In the moment, it seemed plausible, especially with the steep staircase.

After their short investigation, the police left. They took Kim's kids with them. We locked up her house and went to the hospital. She was in St. Joseph's. That first night was one of the longest nights of my life.

She had a fractured skull and severe swelling and bleeding on the brain. She was comatose. Doctors wouldn't let us back to see her. They were struggling to save her. They tried everything, even emergency brain surgery. We waited in the ICU waiting room.

We arrived at the hospital between 6:30 and 7 p.m. and they finally let us see her around midnight. She had all sorts of machines going, with tubes in her mouth, arms and head. I can still hear the steady beeping of her heart monitor and the sound of the medical ventilator keeping her breathing. Her head was mostly wrapped with bandages, but she had a large gash with metal staples I could see. The bright fluorescent lights constant buzzing made me queasy.

My father played the perfect boyfriend in front of the hospital staff. Asking all the right questions and keeping up appearances. He wanted to know what was going on, why her head was swollen, what they were doing to stop the internal bleeding on her brain, and whether she'd come out of the coma soon. It made me sick to be there, mostly because we were living a lie. My dad pushed this poor woman down the stairs with the hope, in the moment, to cause her pain. He got what he wanted. Now here he was, consoling her, holding her hand, and crying into her ear, whispering that she was "going to be alright." I wanted to yell: "You did this to her!" But I just stood there, quiet in the corner.

After about 90 minutes of standing there, watching dad talking to Kim, a nurse walked over.

"Sir, you're going to have to leave the ICU. Visiting hours are over."

We left, but we didn't go home. We slept in the waiting room that night. We weren't the only ones. There was an older couple, in their sixties, waiting, stone faced. I didn't talk to them, but after hearing them speak to each other, I heard the wife mention their son's terrible car crash. It was heartbreaking, though it helped take my mind off what was going on with Kim.

At about 2:00 a.m., I fell asleep. The waiting room TV showed CNN, talking about the 1999 Woodstock summer music festival. I kept falling in and out of sleep in 20 minutes spurts. My mind was racing and the seats were uncomfortable. Dad shook me awake around 6 a.m.

"Hey boy, let's go for a walk," he said.

I didn't want to go, but I didn't say no. Dad never sat still for long. We walked down the long corridor with generic pictures of nature on the walls – deer in a field, birds flying over a sinking sun, and one with rolling hills under a blue sky. We reached the end of the hallway where the elevators stood. Dad hit the button to take us down. I noticed some vending machines and I was starving. I asked dad if we could get some food.

"Yeah, when we get back up here, after our walk," he said.

The doors of the elevator opened and the hospital chaplain walked out, nodding and smiling at us. My dad stopped him.

"Excuse me, can we talk?" my dad asked.

"Sure," he said. "Come with me, I can take you somewhere private."

We took the elevator down to a different floor. They shared small talk about the layout of the hospital. My dad said it was a big place. The chaplain agreed, saying "You get used to it." As the doors opened, the chaplain led the way, followed by my father and me. We came upon a set of wooden doors with a cross on them. The chaplain opened one and we entered the small chapel.

"Have a seat," the chaplain said motioning to us both to sit down.

"Now tell me," he said. "Would you like me to pray with you?"

Before he answered the question, my dad blurted out:

"My girlfriend fell down a flight of stairs and is in a coma with bleeding and swelling on her brain."

I had heard the same line many times that night.

"Oh, I'm so sorry," the chaplain said. "That's terrible. Can I pray for her?"

My dad nodded silently.

The pastor began, asking for strength for us and healing for Kim as well as a blessing for the doctors working on her. He went on for about three minutes. When he finished my dad thanked him.

"Do you have holy water?" my dad asked.

"Yes, of course," the chaplain said. "Come with me."

We got up and walked over to the vessel containing the holy water. The chaplain put his hand in the water and touched my father's head, drawing a cross. I felt wrong, dirty, so I turned around and walked out of the chapel, down the corridor towards the other end of the hallway, back to the elevators. I got to the end of that hall, turned around and could see my dad and the chaplain walking out of the chapel.

We didn't attend church in our house. My mother's odd end-of-times preaching, didn't turn me away from God. Her "religion" did, however, turn me away from finger pointing and "Repent! The end is near!"

God had tested me from a young age. Now I felt like I was failing him. Here I was – walking in a hospital waiting for Kim to make it, or not. I blamed myself. I felt like I was in purgatory. I was battling the cognitive dissonance of everything going on. I was slowly realizing my father's evil and was worried about how easily I could become him.

I was complicit, so I felt evil too. I went along with this lie. I felt as if I was going to go to jail for lying about what had happened. I deserved to. I felt it was my obligation, above all, to protect my father – family comes first. I felt conflicted between protecting him and doing what was right, telling the truth. But I swallowed my conscience and continued walking.

By the time I got back to the chapel, my dad and the chaplain had stopped talking. Dad shook his hand and walked towards me. Since he didn't sleep the night before, he looked haggard. We went back into the hospital chapel to pray. When we got there, we sat in a pew in silence for about a half hour. Then we went to the waiting room to wait for visiting hours to start. Once they began, we sat in Kim's room for about two more hours, until the nurses got annoyed with my dad's questions.

We went back to the waiting room and I fell asleep sitting against the wall, watching more CNN. I woke up and saw my dad talking with an older gentleman in the hallway. He was skinny, with white hair and a mustache. I didn't know who he was. I walked out of the waiting room to the hallway to see what was going on. My dad introduced me.

"Brandon, this is Kim's step-father," my dad said.

"Nice to meet you," I said, shaking his hand.

I could tell he was uneasy. Perhaps he already knew the truth or suspected it. I didn't ask. I stood there frozen.

"So, how long have you two dated?" he asked my father.

"About three months, now," he answered.

***

The debacle started on a Monday. One week after the fall, Kim's condition hadn't changed. She still suffered brain bleeding and swelling. The medicine hadn't stopped either issue. By this time, my father had been barred from visiting Kim's hospital room by her family. We found out her father had worked in some capacity for the FBI before retiring, so he had plenty of law enforcement connections. And her sister was a lawyer who later became a judge. The next day, the family filed a protection order against my father. The week before, hospital staff barred my dad from the premises for sneaking in the ICU rooms after hours, and not following rules.

Monday the 23rd was the first day of eighth grade for me. I looked forward to spending all year in one place. I tried to process everything that happened the week before. Add to that dealing with my father who wasn't sleeping, wasn't eating, and endlessly driving around and listening to music. At least dad stopped making me go along with him. I stayed home. I didn't want to deal with being around him, scared about what my father might say or do. Dad had nothing to lose. This frightened me.

The first two days of school went by without a hitch. The real work didn't really start until the second week. The best part of the first few days of school at Omaha Public Schools in the late 90s was the school lunches. They always gave huge submarine sandwiches with chips the first week. I loved those sandwiches.

On Wednesday that week, I went to Biology class first, then Gym class. Teachers gave us our gym uniforms for the year, ugly red uniforms with "Norris Jr High," spelled out on it. After class I went to German II, which was in a portable classroom section of school, outside. I got into

70

class and the bell rang. This teacher was tougher than the others, and we had a silent quiz that day to give her an idea of what we understood about the German language. As I was finishing my quiz, I heard footsteps walking up the ramp to the classroom door outside. I noticed the shadow of a person shining through the windows. The door opened. It was an office attendant student worker. She had a note for the teacher. Before a word was spoken, I knew Kim was dead. She handed the note to the teacher.

"Brandon McDermott," the teacher said, looking around the room for me. "You need to go to the office."

I gathered my things, walked to the front of the class to grab the office note and made the long walk to the office. After I left the portable room, I walked down the ramp and looked at the note. It read "Brandon McDermott, come to the office."

My heart was racing. Every step along the way, my thoughts ran wild. Who was picking me up? Was it my mom? Was it the police? Am I going to jail? Could it be grandpa? "Please let it be grandpa," I thought. I was about halfway to the office when the front door of the school opened. It was my father. He looked like he had been crying heavily. His face was red and his hair was messy.

"Kim died, let's go," he said, straight to the point.

We walked silently to the car. I didn't say a word. I was still scared he might do something. When you back a man against the wall and he has nothing to lose, there is no telling what he may do. This was the same man who told my mother just weeks before that he would cut me up into a million pieces and that no one would ever find me. We got into the car, he started it up and the stereo blared *"When I See You Smile,"* by Bad English. It was Kim and my dad's song. He must have been listening to this over and over before picking me up. The radio was playing full blast. He turned it off right away.

He always liked to sulk. Now his sulking had made him believe he was the victim in all this.

"They killed her," he said. "They pulled the plug on her. I was in the room with her last week and felt her squeeze my hand twice when I asked her if she loved me."

In that moment, I felt low, I felt sick. He was blaming the doctors, the nurses and Kim's family for her death. Denying all responsibility to the end. I was mad at him and wanted to stand up to him, but I didn't. I just sat there.

"She would've made it, if they only gave her a chance," he said.

They did give her a chance, ten days' of chances. The doctors tried everything they could.

I couldn't believe he wasn't facing any bit of the reality he had caused. Three children were without their mother. Two of them would have trauma for the rest of their lives after what they witnessed. Here he was, this little man, rejecting any accountability for what we both watched him do.

"The police are going to be coming for me. You need to tell them what we told them that night, that she fell. You better not let me down, boy," my dad said.

When he said that I thought, "What about me? I'm going to go to jail too."

He'd let me down for 13 years of life, in a myriad of ways, and he needed me to stand up for him. He spent my whole childhood causing chaos and disrupting my life. Now he wanted to count on the son, he didn't even believe in. In that moment, I wished this was all a dream.

Chapter 12 – Reckoning

Soon after dad and I got home, we heard a knock. I knew who it was. My father opened the door.

"Hello," a cleanly dressed man holding out a badge asked my father.

I could see his holster as he extended his arm.

"Yes, that's me," my father replied.

"I'm with the Omaha Police Department. Where is Brandon?" the man asked.

He was accompanied by a woman detective, who had long reddish-brown hair. She was slender and tall, taller than the male detective – maybe it was her heels.

The woman saw me standing behind my father, in the kitchen, peeking from behind the wall. She entered the apartment as my dad stepped back and she walked over to me. My father let her in, knowing what was happening. Though dad was somewhat wrong. They weren't there for him. They were there for me.

"Brandon, take me to your room," the female detective said to me.

I led her back to my bedroom. She slowly closed the door behind her.

"Honey, you need to pack a change of clothes," she said.

I didn't know what to think. I knew this was going to happen, but somehow I was still in disbelief.

"How many should I take?" I asked. "Should I take anything else too?"

"No, you won't need that. You'll be back to get the rest later," she said.

I packed my favorite Nebraska Cornhuskers t-shirt that my grandma had bought me for my birthday that year. I took a pair of shorts, socks and underwear. The male detective was still talking to my dad when we made our way out of the bedroom and entered the living room. I heard him say they considered dad taking me from school as kidnapping. I walked out of my bedroom into the living room. It was always cold there. My dad kept the A/C very low, especially in August. Dad had the curtains drawn, so the sun couldn't get in. My father's head hung low as I walked towards the door. I felt sorry for him, but I also loved him. I went to hug him, but the woman pulled me back.

"We don't have time for that. We need to go," she told me hurriedly.

I'm not sure he was in the state to give or receive a hug anyway – he looked like he had been hit by a brick. He was ghost white. We left the apartment, the last time I would ever see the place. There weren't any good memories there, not any bad memories either, but it was a place my dad was depressed, obsessed and neurotic. I didn't know where the detectives were taking me. I also didn't want to leave.

The detectives put me in the back of their car, an unmarked black sedan. The leather seats burned my hands when I got in. So did the metal of the seatbelt as I put it on. As we drove away, they poked and prodded me about what school was like, what music I liked and my favorite sports teams. They were trying to break the ice and earn my trust. I knew, even then, that this was a sham. I was scared. They asked me if I was hungry.

"Oh yeah," I said, never one to turn down free food.

"How does Burger King sound?" the male detective asked.

"Sounds fine to me," I said.

As I've said, anytime the police offer you food, it's a bad sign. They were fishing for information and trying to get on my good side. We went to the drive through and I ordered my favorite Burger King sandwich of all time – "The BK Broiler," which they no longer make. They took me to their office in downtown Omaha. We walked through several doors, through offices, and they sat me in a room with no windows. The room had a single clock on the wall. It read 1:30 p.m. The three of us ate lunch together at the table. Then, they started to ask me more about my dad.

"Brandon, we know your dad was abusive. We know he hits you and is verbally abusive," a detective said. "We have the records from when you were in foster care in 1993. It's extensive...what you told us about him then."

I slowly nodded, finishing the French fries I was eating.

"Yes, he beats me," I said in no uncertain terms. "He hits me a lot, calls me names, and makes fun of me in front of people."

I was 13 and had no idea about my rights to counsel – to have an adult and lawyer with me. They were well aware of this fact and never offered me either.

"How often does he hit you?" a detective asked.

By this time, three other detectives stood in the room with us. One sat at the table. The two others stood.

"Every week...sometimes daily," I said.

"Has he ever hit Kim?" they asked.

"No," I said honestly, knowing what they were trying to get at.

"Are you sure?" they asked.

"Yes, I'm sure." I answered.

They asked many more questions, asking about the night my dad pushed Kim down the stairs.

"How did Kim go down the stairs?" they asked.

I told them the lie my dad crafted about how she fell down the stairs. I had to concede that they were arguing because of the holes in the wall. There was also the Pepsi sprayed on the walls and the ravioli all over Kim when they found her. I stuck to my story that, yes, they argued that night, yes, she was kicking us out of the house. However, I lied and said that she went downstairs in such a hurry that she slipped, tripping on the loose metal separating the linoleum from the carpet in her house.

I kept that story up for a very long time. They kept me in the room alone for 90 -minutes at a time. They came back to question me in rounds. Many hours passed. Around 11 p.m. that night, a different detective sat down with me. He put on the tough guy routine.

"Brandon, I gotta tell ya, this looks cut and dried," he said. "Our doctors say there is no way that Kim could've fallen like she did, with the amount of force she had, without being pushed. This looks like you and your dad premeditated this whole thing."

My heart sank to my stomach. It wasn't some sort of pure, selfless decency that caught my ear or my heart. It was my future in question.

"If you don't tell us the truth you and your dad will go to jail for the rest of your lives," the detective said looking me in my eye, like I was a murderer.

I gave up the ghost. I spilled the beans and told them everything. I told them the truth. Point-by-point – everything I've spelled out in this book about that night – I told them. It took about an hour to tell the whole story. They asked questions at every turn, every sentence it seemed.

I was so hungry. I hadn't eaten since when they brought me in at 1:30 p.m. I looked at the clock, it was 1:15 a.m. now. Nearly 12 hours since they brought me in. I asked for food. They brought me some a package of peanuts and a nutty bar. This vending machine food wasn't as nice as the time I last visited the police station, but I scarfed it down nonetheless.

I thought we were done – far from it. They brought in a tape recorder and had me spell out everything is greater detail – down to the channel the TV was on the night of the fight, what shirt I was wearing and where each of the kids were when Kim was pushed down the stairs. It was about 4 a.m. when we finished. I couldn't think, I felt exhausted. I wanted to go home. That was not to be. I remember leaving the station in the middle of the night, after the questioning. Two patrol policemen who weren't part of the questioning, led me out of the building and drove me to a discrete building on 42nd and Center in Omaha with the words "Family Service" lit up brightly on the outside. I found out later it was a youth shelter. They checked me in at the front desk. It was dimly lit and quiet. As the policemen left, the only man there, a twenty-something man at a desk, silently took me to a room with four bunkbeds. He pointed to the top bunk, and I climbed up as quietly as I could. I tried not to wake the other kid sleeping on the bottom. Four other kids were fast asleep in the room. I still remember staring at a poster with cars on the wall that night with the light from a streetlight outside shining on it. I tried to fall asleep as I softly cried thinking about what I had just done. I didn't know where I was, where I was going or when I'd see my family again.

Chapter 13 – Miss The Beat, You Lose The Rhythm

Some kids at the youth shelter had been kicked out of school for selling drugs. Some got into many fights or had problems with truancy. These were problem kids, one step away from the youth detention center. They fought the adult workers and each other.

There was also an 18-month-old child whose parents had meth addictions, and she was born with it in her system. Other than this little child, I was the only other kid there because of our parent's problems.

All of us lived on a point system like what kids at Boys Town live on. You get 100 points for positive interactions with peers and adults. Adult workers give these at their discretion. Being nice and holding a door, giving a genuine compliment – you get 100 points. If you don't listen to instruction, call someone a bad name, or show attitude, you lose 100 points. At the end of the day, you turn in your card which would dictate your privileges for the next day. It felt like a small jail for kids.

I was there because my dad killed his girlfriend. I internalized that. I was paying for my part of Kim's death. I didn't push her down the stairs, but I always felt that I was just feet away, within yelling distance. I could've yelled "Dad, NO!" and it would've stopped him. She would have lived, I thought. That went through my mind for two months, as I lived alone at the shelter. During those two months, I wasn't allowed to leave the premises. The State of Nebraska withheld me from school, worried my father would be bailed of out jail and "kidnap" me again. At least that's what my caseworker told me.

During this time, I couldn't contact *anyone* in my family. Not my parents, not my grandparents, not my aunts or uncles – no one. No phone calls and no letters. The emptiness was immense.

I had to turn to myself at such an early age, that I forget most people don't understand what I lived through. Not having a strong parental figure to lean on for positive life lessons or love and affection was tough. It built a strong urge to do things my way. When I was young, I rebelled. I fought fellow students and didn't listen to teachers or guardians. Part of this was for attention. The other part grew from the fact that I had no structure when dad wasn't walloping me into submission. It meant I could roam freely. Many adults didn't understand that. By age 13, after Kim's death, I knew what I didn't want to be: like my father. While I still loved him, and wanted to make him proud, I knew his lessons were more than bad ones; they were evil. His actions caused me to lose school time and now I was locked up, just like him.

I felt I had to create my future – I had to find, for myself, something to live for. I found my meaning in the best memories I had with my dad – 80s rock music and Husker football.

Because I couldn't go to school, I had to go to my bedroom for quiet time – an hour every day we spent in isolation. I wasn't allowed to take a nap, but if you were good enough and earned enough points you could get a radio.

Every day for 90 minutes, I would listen to CD 105.9 and Z-92, two FM rock stations in town. The music was one of the only links to my father. At that time, I knew he had done wrong, there was no mistaking that. But, I thought he'd get better, because that is what people did when they went to jail. He had to, right? In prison, people had time to think about what they did, and they came out better than before. This was my thought process.

The music he made me listen to for years and years – Lynyrd Skynyrd, Boston, Rush, Styx, Van Halen, Queen, Foreigner and all the other bands – helped save me at the youth shelter. I knew their catalogues – note for note.

I found meaning in the meaningless. I created an arbitrary "Top 500 songs of all time" list. It just happened to be the 500 songs I knew. It didn't matter. Those songs *had* impacted me – they were fundamental to my childhood, good or bad. Every day another song would come back to me. I'd recall sitting with dad in the car listening to it, and I'd write it down on my list of top songs. Soon the list was filled in. I felt like I had done something with purpose. Something that was mine.

Dad and I spent endless hours together. I was practically his right-hand man down the road to madness, stalking his ex-girlfriends. Before we left for a night of stalking, he'd ask me what CDs I wanted to bring along. We'd take six every night. He chose three and I chose three. At the shelter, listening to these songs again on the radio brought me back to better memories.

He instilled the ability to master lyrics and remember useless musical facts. When we'd drive together, he'd quiz me.

"Hey boy, quick," he said in a hurry. "Guess this song before the singer starts singing."

"*Fame* by David Bowie," I said, proud. "That's easy!"

"Good boy," he said.

It was the only time he would complement me. The quizzes were quick, random and obscure.

"Hey boy," he said during the drive around town, "Who is this band?"

Or,

"Who was the first singer of AC/DC?"

Sometimes I'd get it wrong. He liked those times because then he got to be a know-it-all. But I soaked up all his knowledge of music. He loved classic rock and didn't deviate much from that. He was a simple-minded person and his rigidity spilled out into his musical tastes.

The more I learned about obscure and forgotten '80s bands, the closer I felt to dad. Where music drove my father further into his madness, it kept me sane. It was also a memory of my father that wasn't so terrible. I could think of him, with these songs, and not have to remember the beatings or name-calling.

***

The binding to my father, through Husker football, was solidified in the January 1995 Orange Bowl. Nebraska faced off against Miami. We were at Debra's apartment in Papillion. Nebraska didn't play very well to open the game, but they clawed back and dominated the 4th quarter, winning 24-17. After the whistle went off ending the game, I saw my father standing in front of the TV, crying.

"Dad, why are you crying?" I asked curiously.

"I've been waiting for 14 years for this moment," he said. "It's surreal."

When the Huskers did well, we celebrated together.

Dad's love of Husker football was tribal. He wasn't into politics or patriotism, so Husker Football served as tradition and a way of life. We watched games on TV or listened to them on the radio every single week.

Not all Husker football memories were great. Both on the field and in my house. During the 1996 Arizona State-Nebraska game, he was the same old dad. We watched the game at grandpa's house where we lived.

Nebraska wasn't playing well. They had won 26 games straight and hadn't lost in nearly 1,000 days. My father became angry.

"C'mon, fuckin' Huskers! What they fuck are you thinking? He was wide-fucking-open, for fucks sake!" he yelled.

When his temper shot up like that, I knew to tread lightly. He always looked for an outlet. He noticed I had spilled a little soda on the living room table.

"Boy, get a fucking towel and clean this shit up!" he yelled at me. "Are you fucking stupid? You knew it spilled. Why didn't you wipe it up? You're just as clumsy as your fucking mom! This ain't your mom's place!"

He pushed me to the ground, standing over me, kicking me with each sentence. I cowered beneath him.

"Get up!" he screamed. "Get the fuck up!"

As I got up, he slapped me in the back of the head and I began to cry.

"You're crying now?" he asked. "I'll give you something to cry about, boy!"

I ran to the kitchen to get a towel to wipe up the mess.

Later in the game, Nebraska was still playing terribly.

"Goddamn it, what the fuck were you thinking!?" he yelled throwing the remote across the room, nearly hitting the TV.

It smashed against the wall, the batteries flying out.

As Nebraska's offense continued to sputter, dad's remarks grew more pointed.

"Come here! Now, sit the fuck down boy!" he said. "You're fucking up my focus!"

He walked over grabbed me by the shoulders and slammed me into the living room's chair.

"Now stay right fucking there, don't you move a fucking muscle!" he said.

Nebraska fumbled the ball over to Arizona State.

"You fucking idiot!" he yelled at the TV. "Hold on to the goddamned ball!"

He noticed I was sitting on the chair sideways, with my feet flung over the side – my legs waving back and forth.

"Brandon quit your fucking fidgeting. Come sit next to me!"

As I walked slowly over to him, he decided he was angry at my speed. He snatched me by the arm and tossed me on the couch next to him. I picked myself up and I sat down. He put his index and middle finger into my collarbone, forcing me down. Sitting next to him was the place you never wanted to be when his temper was firing on all cylinders.

Nebraska continued to struggle. My dad flipped the plate in front of him off the table. Chips and pizza flew everywhere. I was mad he was taking this out on me, so I gave out a chuckle.

"You think this is fucking funny boy?" he yelled at me, slapping me in the face. "Get the fuck out of here. Go to bed now!"

I got up to walk out and he kicked me as I passed him, knocking me to the ground. I ran upstairs and jumped in bed, crying myself to sleep. My father was taking the loss out directly on me. I thought to myself, "I hope Nebraska loses by 100!"

***

During my time in the youth shelter, I made sure I earned all the points I could to get TV privileges. I wanted to watch the Husker games with the hope my dad was watching them too. Even though watching the games wasn't fun if Nebraska lost, they rarely did, so it was usually respite from the abuse. Just like the music that brought me and dad together, the Huskers brought me closer to him in my mind.

These Saturday's not only passed the time faster, they gave me meaning when my life was spinning in a downward spiral. I could watch the Huskers run over the competition. Watching those games kept my mind on something other than all I had gone through and my current situation. No matter what was happening Sunday to Friday, on Saturday, I could count on the Huskers to put on a shellacking of the opposing team, giving me something to have pride in and something to believe in.

Throughout high school, Husker football helped soothe and still my troubled waters. I could always count on them. No matter what was happening around me, for three hours, 12 or 13 times a year, I could be a part of something larger than myself.

Chapter 14 – Points Counted

While at the shelter, I met with four prospective foster families. Each of them took me out for lunch, a long drive, and a visit to their homes. They asked me questions about my childhood, my interests, my hobbies, and my favorite foods. We went into their homes, where I was showed where my new room would be. Then they showed me the family rooms, the dining rooms, and the back yard where I'd play with my new foster brothers and sisters. One lady sat me down and talked to me directly about my past. Here was this 60-year-old lady talking to a 13-year-old boy like I was a man. She read my file; she knew my past. We were basically having negotiations:

"If you live here, you cannot watch porn. You cannot talk to the other boys and girls about porn. I know what you've gone through, and I don't want you sharing that with any of them," she told me.

I had real hope I would go to this house, that this would be my family. A few days later, Joanie, a worker at the Family Service shelter called me up to the desk. She asked me if I wanted to talk to her for a minute. I said yes, I could see she wanted to tell me something.

"The woman that took you out to her house a couple days ago just called," she said.

She paused for a moment, not knowing how to say the tough part.

"She denied taking you as a foster child at her house," she said. "I'm sorry honey."

I was heartbroken. I couldn't talk to my mom or dad or my family and now strangers were turning me down.

"What about you, Joanie?" I asked, knowing the answer.

Joanie was a nice woman with a husband. They were empty nesters. Their two kids were grown and lived out-of-state, and she lived in a big house. She often said that she would love to have me move in with her, to be my new mom, if the circumstances were different. She was the nicest person at the shelter. She listened to my stories of home, heard them all, and she cried with me. I felt a real motherly connection with her. She cared. But I knew she couldn't take me with her.

"Brandon, you know I would if I could, but I work for the state. They won't let me take you."

I didn't know how the system worked, but I wanted it to work – I wanted something to go my way. Joanie, even though she didn't adopt or foster me, was a big help during those two tough months.

There were two other families who took me out for dinner and talked to me about my past. After an hour or so, they dropped me back off at the youth shelter and I never heard from them again. They were all worried about my past, the trauma I carried and the potential havoc I would wreck on their homes.

***

Many of the workers at the youth shelter weren't mean, per se, but they had to deal with a lot of trouble. It was, in the end, a job for them. Some saw the deeper meaning they could be a part of, helping kids like me in need of love and attention. It was tough, though. Some kids broke out in the middle of the night to smoke weed and get drunk. Some brought drugs in to the center. Some fought the workers. Cops were often called. It was a tense environment. There were lots of fights, adolescents pounding their chests, dealing with their trauma in the only way they knew how – leading with their fists. One teenage boy and girl had sex every chance they could get. In bathrooms, in each other's rooms. Whenever and wherever they could find time and a secret place. They

86

were finally caught, and the boy left. We never heard from him again. There were terrible break ups in there too. People wildly and openly shared grievances before the entire group about each other.

If you received negative 500 points in an hour, it was called an "intensive," which meant that all the kids had to go to their rooms, lock the doors and you had to talk with the worker to de-escalate the situation. It never worked. Intensives made the other kids mad, because they were in effect punished for the anger of one other kid. If the workers were unable to calm the kid down and they continued to not listen, police were called and the kid was never seen or heard from again.

A lot of the kids had loads of trauma. Some had terrible childhoods just like me. Parents who didn't want them, broken homes. Some didn't even know their parents. Many had some serious behavioral issues. I know three of the boys served time behind bars and one guy is still in prison for armed robbery. It was a place for hope where it could click for kids. If it didn't click, they were sent to the Douglas County Youth Center (DCYC) in Omaha. Some kids saw the end of the tunnel and got to go back home. I always felt good for them. It was nice to see them happy on their final day, packing all their belongings and meeting their families to leave. Others didn't last long in the Family Service shelter before going to DCYC.

Some kids shared a bedroom, with three or four others. We were often moved around so we didn't get too familiar with one another. The rooms were strictly segregated by gender. One guy I roomed with was named Frank. He was a Black, British 17-year-old guy who was gay. At first, people made fun of me for rooming with him and called me gay, too. The other kids called him all kinds of slurs, but he was a strong guy, both physically and mentally. He let those slurs bounce right off him. I asked him a lot about his life, where he was from and the like. He was from Southwark, a borough of London. His mom moved to America with a new man after she divorced his dad. Frank came with them at age 14. He got into trouble a lot, he said, after moving to America. He didn't like his mom's new boyfriend and apparently the man didn't like Frank much either. So, Frank left home after moving across the pond and lived on his own for years. He said he lived with a 22-year-old guy for two years, before the guy kicked Frank out. He said they were sexually intimate while they lived together. After leaving, he became a ward of the State of Nebraska. He liked the theatre and could dance and sing very well. He was always singing. He listened to my stories without being judgmental. Yet, he knew I was 14-years-old, and much less mature. He was a good friend in the short time I got to know him.

I entered the shelter on Aug. 27, 1999. I spent a little more than three months there. In November, I received a visit from a heavyset woman named Heather. She had red hair and she was loud and opinionated. It didn't take me long to realize what she was: a prospective foster parent. She took me out for dinner and asked me questions about myself, my childhood and what I liked. Much like the previous women did. She came off very abrasive and pushy. But I didn't care. She showed me attention and seemed to take a liking to me. Plus, after dad, I wasn't worried about what any adult could do to me. She was the fourth person to show interest in me as a possible foster child.

This visit was the shortest of the people who interviewed me. It lasted maybe 30 minutes. We didn't even leave the youth shelter. I thought nothing of it. I figured I'd hear a few days later she wasn't interested or I wasn't "the right fit." But this wasn't the case. The next day, I learned I was moving out of the shelter and into her house. In the moment I felt jubilation. I would be able to go outside again and finally go back to school. Plus, someone heard my story and *chose* me. I remember the ride home to Heather's house. It was in a nice middle-class neighborhood where Bellevue and Omaha meet at the county line. She had a nice three-bedroom house with a finished basement, and three foster kids: a Black teenager named Terrance, a four-year-old girl and me. Terrance and I happened to be the same age. I went to Bryan Junior High school, after missing two months of school, but I didn't have to retake eighth grade, thank goodness.

Heather lived with her husband Todd and her son Mitch, his wife Audra, their 10-month-old son and a family friend named Jeremy. The other foster child, the 4-year-old girl, was very malnourished. She was abused by her mother, left in her crib and she never learned to talk. So she spoke in noises like a baby.

At first, it was great. I got new clothes and shoes. It was the first time in my life I looked clean and felt fresh at school. Usually I wore old shoes with holes in them or shirts two sizes too small. My biological mom usually did our start of the school year shopping at the Salvation Army, if it happened at all.

It wasn't long before I realized this foster home was nothing like Pat's house, where I lived when I was seven and eight. Where Pat showed love and affection, Heather showed disdain. I was used to it as the son of my father, but this was different. I was treated like trash, because in their minds, I was. Heather used to put my mother down for being poor and not having a house to live in.

"There's a reason you're here, Brandon," she said. "No one wanted you and your mother didn't even put the work in to get you back. We'll see if she ever does."

I didn't argue with her or push back, because her sons Mitch, who lived with us, and Pat, who didn't, would smack Terrance and me around. Mitch was in his late twenties and Pat was a couple years younger. Terrance and I did all the house chores. We cooked and cleaned the kitchen, took out the trash, did the laundry for everyone in the house, swept and mopped the floors, vacuumed, dusted, and were all-around indentured servants. Terrance and I did everything they asked of us, from cooking and cleaning to odd jobs, like fetching glasses of water, walking to the store for food, mowing, and shoveling snow. Instead of paying us, we paid them – indirectly as wards of the state. We were for all intents and purposes Cinderella without the ball.

Heather constantly berated Terrance for being poor and Black and for having a drug-addicted mother. How she treated the little 4-year-old girl who couldn't speak made me furious.

The girl tried talking to Heather:

"Gung-ginh! Gung-ginh!"

"You retard we can't understand you!" Heather yelled, pushing her to the ground.

The young girl was small for her age, as she was emaciated when the authorities found her. Heather and company all started calling her "Gung-Gung," because it was what it sounded like the little girl was trying to say. She was a sweet girl. She just wanted love and never got it –from her biological mother or Heather. When no one else was around or they were all asleep, I'd get her out of bed to watch Looney Tunes cartoons and we'd eat cookies and milk. She loved that.

Heather's son Pat made Terrance and me work for him on roofing jobs. We worked for 10 hours a day over three weekends picking up nails and old shingles in the yard of a house they were working on. It was hard, dirty work and we didn't get any pay for it. We only got fast food lunches as payment. Pat, just like Mitch and their mom, verbally abused Terrance and me, calling us lazy, picking on Terrance for being Black and me for being fat. At least I could change being fat. Terrance took it in stride.

"Fuck these rich motherfuckers!" he would say to me as we picked up nails on our hands and knees from tall grass.

He knew our time there was short. Terrance had been in and out of foster homes for three years and was used to the ups and downs of different homes.

The abuse did wear on us though. I hated being around Heather and her family as they didn't care for the foster children at all. They didn't give us any emotional support. We were a paycheck to them. We were their rentals who would cook, clean and wait on them hand and foot.

I stayed there from November of 1999 to late April 2000. In March of 2000, I received word that my mother got a job and a house in North Omaha. I remember sharing the good news with Heather.

"Hey Heather, my mom got a new house!" I said with glee.

"Brandon, it's not a new house – and it's not your mother's house." she said. "It belongs to the landlord and it's in a bad neighborhood. She'll never be able to *buy* a house."

She not only wanted us to do her dirty work, she wanted to remind us that we were less than her and that we wouldn't ever be better than that. When I left her house, there was no party, no congrats, no hugs.

"When you do your packing to leave," she said two days before I left, "make sure you only take what you brought with you. All the clothes you were given or toys you got from us for Christmas and your birthday aren't yours. They are mine. They stay here."

That was one of the last things she said to me before leaving. I came with three or four changes of clothes and that's exactly what I left with – enough to fill two small grocery bags. I never saw Heather or her family again. I later found out Heather died in 2010.

Chapter 15 – A Moment Of Clarity

In late June of 2000, I was sitting at my mom's house watching daytime TV. The phone rang. I got up from my spot in front of the TV and answered the call.

"Hello?" I said, not sure who it could be.

"Hey Brandon, guess what?" It was my sister's voice.

"What?" I said curiously.

"Grandpa McDermott met us at ALDI's grocery store. I'm calling you on his cell phone."

I was flabbergasted. I hadn't seen Grandpa in what seemed like ages. When I went into foster care the second time in August of 1999, the State of Nebraska didn't want me to be in contact with my father. When mom got custody of me, she still didn't allow me to contact anyone on dad's side of the family – no aunts, uncles or grandparents.

The call came on the morning of Friday, June 30 and I'll never forget it. After running into my grandfather at the grocery store, my sisters and I hung out with him for five straight days. During the ride over to my grandparents' house, I wanted to say so much. I had been waiting so long to talk to him. I felt so much more mature than I was just 10 months earlier. I said all I could to grandpa during that ride. Grandpa was a great storyteller and he had the heartiest laugh. When you got him to laugh, you felt it in your soul. It was an accomplishment. I missed him and I told him about ten times.

Those five days, he picked us up early in the morning and dropped us off after dinner at my mom's house. We hadn't been to my grandparent's house in 10 months and it seemed like an eternity. In that time, Grandma had gotten an oxygen tank because she was diagnosed with emphysema after smoking cigarettes for 60 years. She also had a nasty fall the past year, breaking her hip and shoulder. When most elderly people fall and break a hip they are incapacitated the rest of their lives. Not Grandma. That's how strong-willed she was. Life was going to happen her way, no matter the circumstances.

Grandpa bought a hospital bed for her and installed it on the first floor of the house. When I was gone, grandma had a hospital stay and in the time she was there, grandpa moved a ton of newspapers, magazines and old clothes out of the house – all stuff she was hoarding. Grandpa knew it would be tougher to get rid of it as they aged. He felt there was no time like the present. When she returned from the hospital, grandma was very angry, but she eventually forgave him.

I thought about being there as a younger kid and how much I had gone through in the past year. I felt like I had made it over the hill of trouble early in my life. I could be happy again, I thought. The nightmare was over. Grandpa spoiled us that week, buying us a big swimming pool for the backyard. He also took us to Toys 'R Us to pick out toys.

During that week, I went down to the basement and I saw all my dad's and my stuff piled in a corner. I saw Dad's stereo system, packaged neatly in the corner on wooden pallets. There were Dad's Nebraska football shirts in an open box piled with his Husker posters all rolled up with rubber bands. Then another thing caught my eye in a box buried beneath some clothes. It was the 1999 t-shirt from the concert that he, Robby and Kim attended the weekend before he pushed her down the stairs. I saw the band names, Sammy Hagar, Paul Rodgers and Blue Oyster Cult inscribed on the front. As I rubbed my fingers across them it hit me, all the emotions from that night, that summer. All of the stalking trips with dad to his exes' houses, the incessant name calling and the beatings – seeing Kim fall down the stairs, her son screaming. I burst out in tears, crying into the t-shirt – guttural, anguished weeping.

I continued shuffling through the belongings I left behind when the detectives picked me up. There was a poster of Stone Cold Steve

Austin, a Head East CD, and clothes that were now too small to fit me. It was a rush of memories.

I hadn't spoken to my father since the day the detectives picked me up. I still hoped my dad would get out of jail relatively soon and emerge rehabilitated. He still hadn't been convicted or sentenced. There was hope he'd get five years, maybe less. His lawyer was confident that he wouldn't get the maximum sentence.

Those five days with grandpa were a whirlwind. It was a reminder of all the summers we had at the house, and a conclusion to my childhood. We ate grandpa's homemade fried chicken, burgers on the grill, summer sausage, cheese, and ice cream sundaes. Usually grandma wouldn't let us eat ice cream until after dinner, but that week she let us eat whatever we wanted.

Grandma was a stickler when it came to rules, and she was a strong-willed woman. While grandpa allowed the grandkids to eat treats often, grandma only gave us one or two. She wanted us to value and savor them. She was mad at me once for chewing up a sucker, instead of sucking on it. We couldn't have dessert, most times, until we finished our dinner. And yes, she saved our plate of food until we returned to eat it. We could leave, go back home to mom's house and then come back a few days, or a week later, and find out grandma hadn't forgotten about the leftover green beans we didn't eat. They were in the fridge covered with cellophane, and she was ready to heat them in the microwave and make sure we ate them. Before we could have a cookie or piece of candy, we had to. It was frustrating then, but now, it seems like it was yet another tiny life lesson. Rules are rules – we may not like them – but we should follow them.

***

On July 4th 2000, we were hanging out at grandpa's house. We had a great feast for dinner. We had BBQ chicken, burgers, and homemade fries. When it was time to leave, I started crying. I couldn't explain why. Part of it was the mountain top experience of being at grandpa's house and having to come back down again to go home to mom's house. We never had to worry at grandpa's place. No adults to abuse you – or pick on you. There was food aplenty and things to do.

The way mom, Bret, and my uncle Barry treated us when we got back home didn't make it easier. They had an inferiority complex. They felt, and acted, like they were less than us. When we got to my uncle's house that night, we got out of my grandpa's green GM truck. I walked around the truck to the driver's side door and gave him hugs and kisses. I must have given him about 10 that night. His breath always smelled like red onions and Dijon mustard. I could see his eyes were deep blue, but he looked tired. I felt his 5 o'clock shadow on my cheek. It rubbed against my face from all the kisses until it burned. I didn't care. I told him I loved him, and I was looking forward to seeing him the next day. He was coming back over at 8 a.m. to pick us up for another day of fun.

We got home from my uncle's house that night and I ran to bed. It was like Christmas Eve – I couldn't wait to fall asleep. In fact, I forced myself to go to be early. I woke up the next morning to the phone ringing. I jumped out of bed, and leapt over my dog Balou, to answer it.

"Hello?" I said seeing it was grandpa's number on the caller ID.

"Brandon?" It was my aunt's voice.

I wondered why she would be at my grandpa's house on a Wednesday morning at 8:00 a.m.

"Honey," she said, pausing.

I could hear her voice breaking on the other side of the phone.

"Grandpa died this morning."

I thought she had misspoken.

"Grandma died?" I said.

We all expected grandma would die first as she was sick, had emphysema, and suffered failing health.

"No, sweetheart, it was Grandpa. You should get over here," she said.

I dropped the phone, running to my mom's room. I pounded on the locked door wailing. Grandpa was dead.

My life had changed in a moment. Sure, I'd been through hell before, but I had something to live for – being with and around grandpa was a magical experience. I was devastated. There was so much more I wanted to tell him and so much for me yet to learn. There would be no more.

***

I spent most of the summer of 2000 at Grandpa's house. At first, after grandpa died, family was everywhere. Cousins, uncles, extended family all came just like when I was a young during Sunday dinners. Everyone would come over. They served large feasts, food for 25 people, plenty of alcohol and great conversations. In my grandfather's eyes, family was the meaning of life. It was the McDermott way. He had created, along with grandma, this entire, strong family and he wanted to enjoy everyone's company. Those two weeks after his death were a lot like that. My uncle from Washington travelled down for the funeral and in many ways took over grandpa's paternal lead in our family, at least for that short time. A bittersweet final hoorah. Even as a 14 year-old-kid, I could sense this family was going in their own directions. All branches of the family were spreading their wings and grandpa's passing was the death knell to those get-togethers. That said, it was a great few weeks, and a fun summer – even with the biggest loss in my life.

All of us had some rough days after grandpa passed. I took it hard. I tried to search for meaning in anything I could find. Did grandpa know he was going to die? We had one week with him, then he passed away. It was as if he was holding out for us, to make sure we were okay and when he saw that we were, he could go. When he passed, he had three pictures in his wallet. A picture of his wife, his kids and a picture of my sisters and me. He never had to worry about his other grandkids. With us, with my father, he had nothing but worry. We were wards of the state, in foster care – twice in my case. His son was in and out of jail and now waiting to find out his future. This, along with my grandmother's health put a lot of stress on my grandfather. He dealt with my father's legal troubles, traveling to see him in jail and wondering what was going to happen to us kids, all while not being able to see us until the last week of his life. Many people in my father's family blamed Dad for my grandfather's death. They saw him as a waste of space, life and air.

When the extended family went back to their normal lives, I was angry. Why did everyone leave grandma alone? My aunt, her husband, and her oldest son would come over to mow the yard, cut the overgrown bushes, spend time with grandma and bring her dinners. But other than them, no one really visited. It made me furious. Looking back, I know they were all grieving in their own ways – shocked that grandpa had died suddenly, even though he was 79. That shock played into their anger towards my father, knowing my dad added weight to my grandfather's burden.

For a few days after he died, I slept in grandpa's bed. Being in grandpa's room always made you feel special. The bed was soft and it still smelled like him. I'd wake up and walk to the outer attic room where grandpa used to sit, watching TV, sipping coffee and reading the newspaper; I hoped he'd be there. He wasn't. Every time I did this, the feeling got worse. I could hear the clocks in the room ticking, along with distant birds chirping outside. But there was a gaping hole in the room and in my heart.

I searched all of his things, looking for answers. At 14, I thought he was all powerful, that he knew he was dying, that he'd leave me a message or a note. I looked at his medication booklet, with notes and dates for every day and night leading up to the morning of July 5th. The night time medicine entry for July 5th was noticeably missing. I searched old files, papers on his desk, letters in a drawer – I found no note to me. There were no life lessons to find, no direction for 14-year-old me, no help after the deluge.

Chapter 16 – Stuck In A Rut

My stepfather had some good in him. When he dated my mother while I was eight, we became friends. I felt like he cared. Even though I'm now a Denver Broncos fan, he was a Kansas City Chiefs fan. Because he liked the Chiefs, I did too. For his birthday, my mom took me to Target to make one of those "self-made" birthday cards in the old machines that let you design your own. I remember making one for him, saying: To the #1 Chiefs fan, my buddy Bret."

As I grew older, we grew apart. He served as our father in many ways, good, bad or otherwise. When we were teenagers and had moved out of the studio apartment and into a rental house, Bret *loved* to eavesdrop on conversations between us kids and my mom. He would stand behind the door in the hallway, listening in, ready to jump in when I said something he didn't like. After these arguments, they'd go back to their bedroom, lock the doors and smoke weed.

My stepdad didn't like us. I think he did at first, but as we reached our teens, we were tough to deal with. Teens don't listen to their parents, much less a step-parent. He wasn't our "real dad," and we surely let him know that. He came to resent us.

The only room in the house with air conditioning was my parent's room, where the dogs slept, and the door remained shut. The "good food" was locked in their closet – the snacks, the soda. They dispersed it to us as they saw fit, like a bread line in the Soviet Union. They said we ate all the food, and my step father had high-blood pressure, so it was most important for him to have air conditioning. On the hottest summer nights, when the air was thick with Nebraska humidity and no wind, I asked if I could sleep on their floor with the dogs. They wouldn't let me.

As I've said, my stepdad was the polar opposite of my dad. He didn't hit us or my mom. However, in other ways, he was a chip off the old block. He couldn't keep a job, verbally put her down and played us kids off my mother. He treated us like we were wasting his time and annoying him for even knocking his bedroom door. He wanted nothing to do with us by the time I was a teenager. We were also a reminder that he, himself, would never have kids of his own.

My stepdad had many jobs throughout my childhood. He worked at Albertson's and Village Inn for a time. He also worked odd jobs, some from the local temp agency. But usually, after a few weeks, we'd hear him laying the groundwork for quitting.

"My boss is playing me. He's not giving me the hours I want," he said. "I'm more than a dishwasher. I could be running that whole place myself.   He's   a   fool."

I could tell when he had a job, because the house had to be "very quiet, so I can get some sleep!" The only way we knew he quit a job was when he stopped complaining about work or asking us to be quiet.

***

Even after my father went to jail and was awaiting his sentence, my mother, and by default, my stepfather, were envious and resentful of my grandparents. They reminded us that they were terrible parents.

Their only competition as loving parents, my father, was in jail and had killed a woman. They didn't have to live up to much, and they hated being challenged. When, as a teenager, I'd argue with them, it was the first thing I always brought up.

"You can't even hold a job!" I told Bret. "You're a lazy pile who sits around, smokes weed, drinks and does nothing else. I bet your mom is real proud."

"Watch your mouth boy!" he said.

I gained my father's ability to throw the kitchen sink at people in the lowest way possible. To hit the right, or the wrong, buttons. I knew he wasn't going to hit me. That was my saving grace, but it also destroyed any chance I'd show respect for either of them. Sure, they could punish me, and they did. I got grounded, but when you've got nothing at home to be grounded from – you don't lose much.

"Does it make you feel like a big man to know my mom has to work and you sit home all day doing nothing?" I asked him.

"I do plenty, boy!" he said back. "I cook, I clean and I keep this place tidy."

"Bret, we have roaches and mice and never have food. Do you feel like a big housewife with *all* that you do?"

He slammed his bedroom door, locking it behind him.

After living in foster care and youth homes, I knew what was *normal* and what was acceptable. I knew what other kids got from their families – even kids who had less money than us, many had loving parents who worked hard and did their best to succeed. Most parents did all they could to set up their kids to do better than they had done. Not my parents.

***

After grandpa died, I brought home a bunch of my old stuff from dad's apartment. Grandpa had given me an old, box 19-inch TV to play my old Nintendo 64 on the week before he died. I needed an adapter for it, so we went to the now defunct RadioShack in North Omaha that week. I was an unruly kid who wasn't afraid to ask for toys from grandpa, and he never shied away from buying them. That week in particular, grandpa was sure to sprinkle his love through gift giving. To this day, I still have the receipt for the adapter. The ink is faded, but you can still read it if you hold it up to the light. When he died, all I had were the memories and the stuff he gave me. Back then, I believed that stuff – the TV, the adapter, the video games – would preserve his memory.

I wasn't easy to be around the summer and fall after Grandpa died. I spent a lot of time listening to the CD Grandpa gave me in fifth grade. It was from John McDermott, one of the Irish tenors. One song in particular always hit me – *"The Last Rose of Summer."* It's a heartbreaking poem, turned song, with a metaphor of the final flower of the summer, signifying the passing of loved ones. I can still hear my grandfather singing it as he walked the halls of his house. He had a lovely operatic tenor voice. After going through his things when he passed, I found an old recording from when he took voice lessons. It was him singing and laughing with his instructor as they sang and played piano. When I found it, I asked grandma if she wanted to hear it.

"No, honey," she said. "I can hear him singing and laughing when I close my eyes."

Twenty years after he passed away, to this day, I can hear his voice singing. I miss it, but I am never too far away from also closing my eyes and remembering it.

Between paychecks, Mom and Bret used to turn to hocking their belongings – jewelry, TVs, video game systems, VCRs, and other household appliances – at the pawn shop in Omaha. One day in September of 2000, I woke up and found my TV, video game system and games were all gone. I panicked. Running upstairs, I saw my mother sitting in the living room with my uncle. As soon as they saw me, they shuffled to get rid of the weed and cheap copper pipe they were smoking out of.

"Mom, where is my stuff?" I asked.

"Honey, we needed to pay rent this month," she said. "Don't worry, we'll be getting it back in three weeks."

I was livid.

"You did what?" I screamed. "My grandpa gave me that! That wasn't yours to hock at the pawn shop. This family is complete trash!"

Her tone changed.

"In this house, your stuff is my stuff," she said, challenging me to shout back. "I put a roof over your head and food in your mouth. We wouldn't have a place to live without that money."

With all the stuff my sisters and I went through as kids, nothing sticks in my craw quite like the jealousy my mother and Bret had for my grandparents. Top that trash salad with mom hocking the last gifts grandpa gave me and it still angers me.

In the end, I never saw that TV or video game system again. She never attempted to get it back, or she couldn't because she didn't have the money. Either mom spent it on cigarettes, weed and beer, or she and Bret didn't have enough funds to get it back from the pawn broker. My grandmother got mad too, but she was also mad at me.

"Your grandfather bought that for you!" she said. "Why would she take that and pawn it? Why didn't you stop her?"

I think grandma knew that there was nothing I could do, I explained they took it when I was sleeping. She was just peeved that my mom would stoop that low and use the excuse of paying rent. In the end my mother claimed to get $45 for the TV and video game system. I never saw a cent of that money.

***

A couple weeks after grandpa died we watched TV at my uncle Barry's in North Omaha. My two sisters, mom, Bret and I showed up around noon and stayed all day. It was mid-July. The adults sat in the dining room yelling at each other about the Bible and smoking weed. If we had to use the restroom, we had to knock on the wall and wait for a response. This time I knocked.

"Who is it?" my uncle yelped.

"Brandon, I need to pee," I said.

"Hurry up boy," my uncle said.

I opened the curtain and walked through the room. It smelled like foul, low grade weed. They always smoked it out of a copper pipe. When we would walk through as kids, they'd shuffle it behind a drink, or under the table, in their pocket and the like. As I got older, I knew what they were doing and they knew I knew. It was foolish to think otherwise. They didn't try hard to hide it. That day I called them out.

"Have you guys smoked enough of that stuff yet? It smells bad in here."

"Shut your mouth boy!" my mom said. "Go piss and get out of here."

My uncle couldn't hold his tongue, partially because he had few teeth. Drugs were rough on him.

"Yeah, we're smoking, is that okay?" he said. "Should I kill my girlfriend, would that be better for you?"

My mom wasn't happy with that.

"C'mon, Barry, leave him alone."

"No, he doesn't want to hear the truth," he said. "Let him hear it. Your dad is a bastard, woman-abuser who will rot in prison."

I was always good with a quip.

"Just like your teeth, right Joe?"

That shut him up pretty quick.

Later that afternoon, Joe made the trip out of his pot induced stupor to come to the living room where his two sons, my two sisters, and I were playing. He turned off the video game that his son Jake was playing.

"Dad, what are you doing I was playing *Donkey Kong*!" he said.

"Shut up, Jake. You can play in a minute," he spat at him.

My uncle smiled like an evil troll with a single tooth hanging out of his mouth. He grabbed a VHS tape from behind the TV and put it in the VCR.

"I've been waiting to show you this," he said slyly.

He changed the channel and pushed play.

"You're not going to want to miss this," he said, grabbing all of our attention.

The tape started playing. It was Rob McCartney and Julie Cornell on KETV in Omaha during a newscast. The tape was a bit grainy.

"Good evening, alongside Julie Cornell, I'm Rob McCartney – and you're watching NewsWatch 7. We've been following the case of an Omaha man who allegedly pushed his girlfriend down the stairs in front of his 13-year-old son and her three young children. The woman later died. The man is being charged with involuntary manslaughter in the woman's death..."

The tape stopped.

"I told you that you wouldn't want to miss it," my uncle said chuckling. "I heard your grandpa died last week. He got what he deserved...he paid for your father's sins..."

"Fuck you, Uncle Barry!" I said. "You're an asshole and no one likes you."

"At least I'm alive and not in jail!" he said.

He turned Jake's game back on and left the room.

I was so mad, I started to cry. I didn't want him to see he got to me. I tried to hide it, but I couldn't. Tears were streaming down my face.

"Need to talk to your mommy, crybaby?" my uncle said, as he closed the curtain.

***

I argued with my mom, asking if we could go home after Barry showed us the recording he made. Mom was mad at me for asking. She was "relaxing," she said and didn't want to leave. But I caused a ruckus and we took the bus home. She yelled at me after we got off the bus. We walked the rest of the way back.

"Why couldn't you have just shut your damn mouth, huh?" she asked.

"I don't like being over there. It's dirty and all you do is smoke."

"Well, you're a kid and I'm the adult. You do as I say, as long as you're under my roof."

"Yeah, you may think you're the boss, but you're not a good one, mom," I said. "At least dad didn't smoke weed all the time."

I was a teenager, quick to remind her that she was at least partially to blame for all the crap that we went through

"I don't understand why you kids love your dad so much," my mother said. "He abused you, called you names, and made you feel small. At least I'm not in jail. I'm here taking care of you."

She wasn't wrong. Perhaps that's at least partially why she was jealous of him and envious of us liking him more than her, when we were young, even though he did all those terrible things.

It always felt like caring for her kids was a burden for my mother. I can't tell you how many times I heard: "Get out of here, leave me alone, and get out of my ass! Go do something!" There were no times we hung out as a family at my mom's house – no watching TV with her, no trips to the zoo or trips to the county fair. It was nothing like being with dad. I think later she came to hate that even though he was locked up, we missed him more than we ever loved her.

Chapter 17 – Uncle Vinnie

My grandfather and father had a large impact on my life. The third man who had perhaps the most direct impact on my adolescence was larger than life. He was belligerent, loud and he shot you straight – whether you asked for it or not. He was my uncle Vinnie.

Vinnie was a cornerstone, too, in how my father was raised. He, along with his twin brother Eddie, were the hell raisers. My dad was their lackey. They got in a lot of trouble together.

They were all thick as thieves, and they actually were thieves. My uncles, Vinnie and Eddie, told me stories of having house parties as teens and robbing strangers of everything they had. When the owner of the house would wake up the next day, they'd find their house completely wiped out of stereos, furniture, jewelry and other valuables. The key, they told me, was to never hold a party at someone's house they personally knew, and to get the homeowner absolutely trashed. It was always the house of a friend of a friend or a girlfriend. So, when the unsuspecting house party host woke up looking for answers, they would not remember a thing, calling people they knew were at the party looking for two fat guys – whom no one could name. And no one ever saw them again.

Another story goes that Vinnie got a girl for my dad to hook up with. My dad, then a virgin, and a scrawny, skinny teenager, was at a party. Vinnie found a willing girl to sleep with my dad. Dad was scared and ashamed to be put on the spot. Dad said Vinnie told him that if he didn't do the deed, that Vinnie would do if for him and make my dad watch. Instead of being considered a "pussy," dad went through with it. Vinnie later told me he was proud of my dad. Dad never gave too many details about what happened that night in the bedroom, with the door closed.

Vinnie was a broken and flawed man, but in some ways he was ten times the man my father was. I believe my father came to hate him for that.

My dad and Vinnie had a falling out several times in the late 80s and early 90s. I never knew what started it but it was more than likely about my dad getting sober. He stopped doing drugs in 1985 and stopped drinking in 1988. Dad had a superiority complex, part of which was lived out by choosing to be around people that made him feel strong and superior. Maybe this was because he grew up as the bullied kid and Vinnie was a bully. As they grew, they became good friends unified by being fellow drunks. When Dad stopped drinking, he had no reason to hang out with Vinnie like they had before.

Dad liked to bring me over to Vinnie's house in North Omaha, every now and then, when I was younger. They rented a huge house with many bedrooms, even though Vinnie's family were poor like us. It was Vinnie and his five kids and wife Leona in the house.

Dad and Vinnie would chat and all of us kids would play. They'd retell old stories and lovingly bag on each other. My dad always had a way to rip on Vinnie about his drinking.

"You know, I gave up the bottle, after all we did back then. You need to too, before it's too late," he said.

"Yeah, I know," Vinnie said to my dad dismissively. "I know the game."

Perhaps dad was trying to save an old friend, but there was also the power he held over Vinnie. While Vinnie couldn't overcome his addictions and demons, dad liked to think he had. Being a recovering alcoholic around a bunch of binge-drinkers boosted dad's confidence and made him feel like a success. He wasn't, he never was. But it was easy to forget, both for him and others, when he was surrounded by people he could manipulate. He couldn't manipulate Vinnie though. He knew his demons well and he never ran from them. I like to think he chased after them with all he had.

Vinnie was at his best in social situations, even as a heavy drinker. He could read people and make them feel like they were his best friend.

This is a calling card for the addicts I've known. They tended to do what it takes to get what the need to fulfill their thirst. Dad learned a lot from Vinnie when it came to reading people and the room. Dad mastered the art of getting what he wanted out of people. He learned it from Vinnie.

Pain and suffering can bring a person wisdom, but it's never worth the price. He grew up poor. His dad was a drunk who beat him, his brothers and sisters, and their mother. My grandpa used to tell us he'd feed Eddie and Vinnie when they came over to his house as young kids because they were living so poor. There's an interesting family tie between Vinnie's family and my dad's. Vinnie's sister is married to my dad's brother. So, Vinnie wasn't my actual uncle, we aren't related by blood, but he was around the family when I was a kid.

***

In 2001, when I was a sophomore in high school, my mother sat me down in her bedroom at the house. Bret was there too. He stood in the corner of the room, his arms folded with a smug look of victory on his face. Mom told me they wanted me to get a job and start paying $200 a month for rent. She said I was an adult and I should start paying my fair share in the household. I stood there, astonished. At 15, I couldn't get a job that would give me enough hours to make much more than what she was asking every month. My arguments fell on deaf ears.

Dad had been convicted of killing Kim just a few months before this. He was charged with involuntary manslaughter and given the maximum in the state of Nebraska of 18-20 years. The judge threw the book at him for having three protection orders and breaking all of them. Add to this his proclivity for abuse of women and children, and the judge wasn't taking any chances.

Mom was angry we wouldn't see any of the back pay from the child support "dad owed her" since my sisters and I would be aged out by the time he was released. Mom wanted me, a 15-year-old boy, to pay my dues. I told them I was having none of that. So, she kicked me out. She tried a couple years later to make me come back, because of how "it made her look as a mother," but I lived on-and-off with Vinnie from age 15 to 17.

Uncle Vinnie and Aunt Leona took me in, no questions asked. In fact, when I brought up what my mom told me, they were overjoyed to have me move in with them. They didn't ask anything in return other than to be a good kid, not cause any trouble, go to church like the other kids, and attend Bible study and youth group every week. Church and youth group were my saving grace.

It was a release from being at my mom's. Like other times as a kid, it felt like a fresh new start. I was able to escape the endless deluge of negativity of mom's house. Sure, Vinnie and Leona were poor, but they had love in their family. It didn't mean there weren't issues, though. I lived in the basement with my cousins Noah and Will. My three other cousins also lived with us. We were perhaps poorer than when I lived with mom. They didn't get more food stamps because of me, as I was living there "off the books." My mother received aid from the state for me, in my absence. Like Bret, Uncle Vinnie didn't have a job. Leona had the only job in the house and money was tight. However, we made the most of it. None of the kids, Vinnie, or Leona ever made me feel bad for being there. In fact, they told me they loved me and wanted me to stay. I felt at home.

My uncle Vinnie drank — a lot. He would binge for days. Literal days. He'd wake up at 10 a.m. and try to find money and company for that binge. This meant asking Leona for cash, or stealing it from her purse. It got so bad that Leona started hiding money in the unused basement fireplace. If he couldn't get Leona to give him cash, or she had none, he'd hit up Eddie, or his other brother and sisters, or a myriad of friends. Once he secured money for the binge, he'd go out and buy beer. He liked Milwaukee's Best Light, Old Milwaukee, or Natural Light. The cheap stuff you could buy a lot of and get wasted easily on. He and Eddie, usually his drinking partner, would stay up and sit on the porch drinking, chain smoking cigarettes and listening to music. When they'd get done with one pack of beer, they'd secure funds for another. And they would stay up and continue to drink.

More than once, I witnessed him puking, not because he couldn't handle his alcohol, but so he could have more room in his stomach for another drink. That was the hold this addiction had on him. Often his kids and I would stay up late with him. He wasn't hard on bed times. We'd go to bed and wake up to him cranking Boston's Greatest Hits on the stereo, him and Eddie still awake and drinking. We'd go to school and come back home and they'd be even more hammered, still binging in a mess of empty cans and cigarette butts. Sometimes this lasted for three days.

When we got older, Vinnie's youngest son, Elijah, grew angry at his dad for his drinking. He started to realize his dad was slowly killing himself. Elijah got to the point that he was stealing his dad's beers and smashing them so he couldn't drink them. One night, this turned comical. Vinnie found his Elijah smashing his beers against the cement in the backyard. Vinnie chased him around the outside of the house, as his son smashed more beers every few feet as he ran beyond his reach.

"You need to quit, dad!" Elijah said. "This is killing you!"

"Boy you better get back here. You're going to pay for every damn one of those!" Vinnie said in desperation.

This continued until the beers were all gone. It didn't matter, Vinnie would always find more money or more people to enable his slow destruction. He turned to hiding the beer in the trunk of the car, until Elijah found them and smashed all of those too. Vinnie finally wised up and put his case of beer in the oven and sat down in front of it. There he chain smoked and drank, taking his beers with him to the bathroom. No one was going to move him and take them now...and they didn't.

***

112

After Elijah grew angry at him for his drinking, all of his sons stopped talking to him. I was the only one who would come out with him to the porch when he drank. He needed and wanted the company. One night in the winter of 2003, all the kids and Leona were gone. It was a cold snowy night. I wondered when anyone was going to come home and I sat on the front porch waiting for them. As the snow fell heavily, I noticed Vinnie's silhouette slowly walking down the street toward the house. Part of Vinnie's attitude about life, his middle finger to the world, he lived through how he walked – in his strut. It was a bit gimpy, but he held his head high with his shoulders back. Even in the snow, he was unmistakable. He walked slowly home. He got to the porch.

"Heh...bouy...c'mere..." he slurred.

I walked over to him and he hugged me tighter than I'd ever been hugged before. He smelled like burned cigarettes, and strong liquor. I noticed he had a brown bag with a bottle of clear liquid, vodka. He never drank hard liquor, unless he was overtly depressed. He was that night. He was slurring his speech, but he wanted me to listen.

"You think I'm stupid...I'm not...I know I got problems..." he said. "...I just can't beat this..."

I felt so sorry for him. I stared into the eyes of the man I looked up to the most at that point. He was at rock bottom. He had quit drinking many times before this – even for long periods, six months or a year. When he did, it was amazing. We thought it was for good. A keg at a Super Bowl party later and he relapsed, hard. He knew there was no going back to recovery at this point. There was no hope left to grasp. He'd tried to get a career, go to church, but none of it ever solved his problems. No amount of alcohol, sobriety, jobs, partying, starting up and quitting it all ever made his problems leave. That was what he was facing and what he couldn't understand or make any of us understand.

There were times when he was coherent and clear as day – even when he was drunk. One night we were on the porch and he told me he was proud of me.

"You're doing good, boy," he said. "Your dad was a fuck-up, beating on you and his women. It wasn't right and you could've gone down the rabbit hole, but you didn't."

I've been given a lot of compliments in my day, perhaps too many, but this one made me feel good. It hit home and I knew it was from the heart. Vinnie didn't play around. He shot from the hip – what he thought, he told you. You always knew you were getting his truth.

"Life's a dream boy, an illusion," he told me one day.

Sometimes he had a way to get at an important life lesson, in a few short words. He passed on much wisdom to me, even though it would never remedy his own suffering.

He passed his "middle finger to the world," onto me. I took all that life threw me and mixed it with his attitude of "I'll show the detractors." He didn't like Van Halen like my dad and I did, in fact he made fun of us for liking them so much. But he loved David Lee Roth's quote:

"I hear you don't like me...do me a favor, pass it on to everyone else."

That's who I am. We were gutter kids. The world had forgotten us and I wanted to make sure they'd always remember. He, like my mom trusted no one outside of family. But family came first – even through his addiction, his sickness. He loved family cookouts and good tunes.

"Go on boy, throw on some jams," he used to tell me when he'd get drunk.

His boys loved newer music, but I loved the classics, rock music like how it should be.

Sometimes when he'd get drunk, he'd call 911 and tell them that he was going to kill himself. I'm not sure if there was truth to that threat or not, but the police took it seriously. One night they showed up, he was holding a knife to his neck, threatening to kill himself and the police. The police blocked off the whole street. They used bean bag rounds, not meant to penetrate or cause long-term damage but they hit hard enough to knock you back and take your breath away. The police were able to save him. He woke up the next day with bruises all over his chest in jail.

Vinnie had no time for what was socially acceptable. He hated authority figures. Whether it was a 9-5 job or climbing the corporate ladder, a religious self-proclaimed authority, landlords or politicians. But he also had no idea about the mental issues he had. He later found out about them from doctors, when it was too late. So he medicated his sickness the only way he knew how and blamed it on the world around him.

***

On February 12th 2006, I stayed overnight with a friend at his grandparents' house. As young, stupid 20-year-olds, we snuck into his grandparents' liquor cabinet and got blasted. I came back to my apartment, where Noah and I lived, the next morning. I was very hung over. When I opened the door, Noah was on ground in the living room on a make-shift bed with his then girlfriend, now wife. He should've been sleeping, but he wasn't.

"Hey man, I've got some bad news," he said waking up to the sound of the door opening. "My dad died last night."

I stood there with the door wide open in disbelief. I went through all of the stages of grief in about two minutes. We all saw it coming, who couldn't? Five years prior, doctors told Vinnie he had five years to live – five years to quit drinking and get himself clean for good. By 2006, he had lost vast amounts of weight, though he still looked fat. When he took his shirt off, you could see Vinnie's big belly hanging over his belt, but you could also see his ribs. His brother, Eddie, his twin and life long-drinking partner, found him face down in his bed after a long night of drinking. He was dead – blue in the face and bloated. He had been drinking heavily like always, but he was also taking different medications to deal with anxiety and depression. They weren't prescriptions; they were "samples" given to him from his doctor. He died five years, nearly to the month, after his doctor originally gave him that warning. He was 45.

The funeral was a rough one for me, right up there with my grandpa's. His kids have it hard to this day, wondering what it all meant, why it all happened like that. I'm still using those lessons, the middle finger to the world, the take me as I come just like he did. I hope he's proud.

Chapter 18 – On Your Own Again

At one point while I was living at Vinnie's they had to move out of the house they were renting. The landlord forced them out. They hadn't paid rent for more than a year and owed more than $10,000. The landlord was an old lady who owned a bunch of residences in North Omaha. She felt sorry for what Leona had to deal with, Vinnie being an alcoholic and raising five kids on one job. She let it slide for a time. But then the old lady died, and her son took the properties. He told them the jig was up. Vinnie didn't take this lightly.

"Fuck him!" he yelled in between puffs of his cigarette. "We're not leaving! He can leave!"

It was ludicrous and funny all in one sentence. He somehow turned his lack of a job and his alcoholism into someone else's fault. We all moved to a family member's basement in North Omaha. I came with them for a time, sharing the basement on three mattresses laid in a row on the ground. Money was tighter than ever. Vinnie told me I had to move back home until they were able to get a house. I was heartbroken, because I knew this was the addiction talking. I was, in his words, eating a lot of food and they didn't have the money for it. The daily beer and cigarettes cost more than I did, but I went home. Mom agreed to let me live there for free for a month, I was 17. It took Leona about a month to find a new place and I eventually moved back in with them.

I graduated Benson high school with a 1.68 GPA in the lowest 1/6th of my class. But in my mind, it didn't matter. I still graduated. I was a first-generation high school graduate and that was a good feeling. I remember the night of graduation, at the Civic Auditorium, Vinnie and Leona were there. So were my mom and Bret. I reluctantly gave the two tickets I had, the good floor seats, to my mom. Vinnie and Leona had to sit in the upper deck. He wasn't happy about this.

"Leona and I raised you, I don't know why you gave your mom the tickets," he said.

He was hurt. He *did* raise me, sat with me on the porch during my first heartbreak and told me everything was going to be okay. He helped me grasp my dad's earliest years and helped me get a better understanding of how my dad ticked. Vinnie saw me through my childhood's true last rite of passage: facing my father's past and knowing I didn't need his sins as I'd come to have my own someday. He saw me through some of the darkest hours of my adolescence. He was a proud man and family meant more to him than it did for both of my parents combined. As an addict, he was notoriously selfish, but he still had the ability to care and give. Neither of my parents did. Not having Vinnie and Leona sit on the floor at my graduation is one of my life's true regrets.

One night in September of 2004, Noah and I were watching old VHS tapes of Van Halen. We loved watching the old concerts. Vinnie was drunk and, on this night, he was drinking alone in the back yard. He came inside to use the bathroom. He saw we were watching Van Halen. He entered during Alex Van Halen's drum solo.

"He isn't that good," he said. "Aerosmith's drummer – he's the best drummer."

Me being the know-it-all that I am, called him out. I took the bait.

"No, he's not," I said. "Alex Van Halen may not be *the best,* but he is better than Aerosmith's drummer. You don't ever know Aerosmith's drummer's name."

"Fuck you, boy," he said. "You got a smart mouth just like your daddy. You don't know shit. That's why your mom is a whore! She fucked another dude while she was still married with your dad."

I was floored. He never said anything like that to me before. While I didn't care much about what he said, and he was technically right, he called my mom a whore and I wasn't going to take that. I got up and ran over to him, got into his face.

119

"Say it to my face!" I yelled at him.

"Your fat ass mommy is a big fucking whore!" he said.

I could smell the beer on his breath and see his eyes were glossed over. He was blinking very slowly.

I pushed him, but before we could fight, Noah came and saved me, pulling me back.

"You're out of here, boy!" Vinnie told me. "Pack your shit. You're leaving tonight."

And with that, I left. It's my personal belief, and my cousin Noah agreed, that he kicked me out because it was less money spent on food I'd eat or utilities I'd use and thus more money to feed his addiction. It was less pressure on the house, and with that, less pressure on him. Within two days, Vinnie kicked out his oldest two sons, too. I tried to go back home to mom's house, but she wanted me to pay $350 a month rent plus split the utilities with her and I wasn't going to do that.

The three of us were homeless for about a week. We slept in my cousin's car. We ended up staying with a friend we knew from church. She heard of our situation and her parents agreed to house us. They set clear rules: we needed to find jobs and move out, though no timetable was given. Two other families came together to help us. They all lived in Millard and were, in our minds, rich kids. They were just upper-middle-class families. One family agreed to pay for our food, one family agreed to pay for things like new clothes and the third family let us stay at their house. We stayed in the basement and were not allowed to go to the second floor of the house – that's where their two daughters stayed.

It turned out to be a huge blessing. The families didn't have to help us, there were community programs we could've sought out for help. However, the three of them belonged to a large church and took their call to give back to their community in a real way. For that I will always be grateful. It was better than sleeping in the back of my cousin's car or outside of a friend's house like we had been doing. The family showed a lot of grace and it was a godsend for us, but Noah and I wanted out. Not because the set up didn't work – we had just happened to be born into a world where our parents got comfortable doing just enough to get by, sometimes without necessities like heat in the house or electricity. We wanted more.

***

Noah and I looked for jobs, walking the Westroads and OakView malls in Omaha for hours. We applied everywhere: Burger King, McDonald's, Runza, and other fast food joints. We applied at Wal-Mart, Shopko, Target, and department stores. No one called us back, perhaps because we were too needy. I woke up one morning and came upstairs to the kitchen to find Noah reading the newspaper and perusing the wanted ads. I noticed he had a few circled in red ink.

"Hey man, check this out," Noah said reading "Travel for free, visit all 48 contiguous states. Never see winter again! 1-888-PAID-FUN..."

"Whoa," I said. "What do you think it is?"

"Not sure, but I think we should at least call them," he said. "I want to get out of this town."

We decided then was as good a time as any. We picked up the kitchen landline and dialed the number. I thought to myself that "a phone number like 1-888-PAID-FUN couldn't be all bad." The phone rang about six times, which was more than usual, as a voicemail machine tended to kick it at ring number four or five.

"Hello?" an old, gravelly-voiced woman answered, clearly out of breath as if she had run to the phone.

"Hello, we saw your number in the newspaper," I said. "We're curious about the job."

"Well thanks for calling, it's a travelling job," she said. "Very easy job. We pay your way out here to where our team is currently located. We travel with the sun, so we are in Philadelphia right now, moving to Boston in two weeks, then down the East Coast until winter. Then we stay south, through Florida, Louisiana, Texas, Arizona and California. Then we move all the way back through the rest of the country after winter ends."

We were both listening to the call, with our ears to the receiver.

"Sounds good," I said. "What would the job be?"

"You'd be door-to-door salesmen, selling magazines," she said. "Also, something to remember, if you don't like that job after two weeks, we will send you back home free of charge."

"So, you'd pay for us to travel to you *and* if we don't like the job, we get to go home for free?" I asked.

"That's right," she said.

At that point, Noah was giving me non-verbal cues to show he was in: nodding and giving thumbs up.

"This sounds very good to us. Can we discuss it a bit and call you right back?" I asked.

"Sure thing, no prob, hun," she said. "Call me back when you decide. Thanks for ringing us."

And with that we ended the call. Noah and I both agreed that this was a good opportunity, not because it would be a long-term job, but because we wanted out of Omaha and were having no luck looking for jobs. There *had* to be better job prospects on the East Coast. On top of this, Noah's love interest went to school in New England. He was sold almost immediately. I wanted to do something – anything – meaningful with my life after all I'd gone through. I thought I was unbreakable. How could I fail? We called the lady back, she took our information and called us back 20 minutes later saying we had two one-way Greyhound tickets to Philadelphia the next day.

We were two young kids with parents who lived impulsively, and we followed their example with a lack of forethought, ready to give up everything we knew for an unknown future. We didn't care. We challenged life to give it to us. We wanted our shot to show the world.

***

Neither of our parents showed at the Greyhound station when we left. But our host parents from Millard showed up and they teared up. They even brought a paper bag of bread, peanut butter, and a few snacks to keep us fed on the way out. They also slipped us $20. It was much needed, as we were dead broke and had no idea how we were going to eat.

We said our goodbyes and walked into the station to get out tickets, arriving at the counter and giving our information. As we approached the window, I wondered "Is this for real, are there really tickets here for us?" There were. They gave us two tickets and we waited for our bus to arrive.

If you ever had the chance to ride a Greyhound bus, you know some of the stations are dilapidated and gross. The station in downtown Omaha, which is now closed, was rather small. It was about the size of a Burger King with a large parking lot for buses to arrive and park. Our bus showed up about 45 minutes after we got there. We loaded our bags to the driver and he threw them under the bus. Then we got on. It smelled like urine and dirty socks. It had dingy, faded seats, but we didn't care. We found the last two seats side-by-side. We had more than 30 hours ahead of us before we got to Philadelphia. By car the trip from Omaha to Philly is about 18 hours. But we had layovers in several cities along the way: Iowa City, Chicago, Cleveland, Pittsburgh and Philly. We left Omaha late at night, around 10:00 p.m. on a Tuesday and we arrived in Philly at 8 a.m. on Thursday.

***

We arrived in downtown Philly at the Greyhound station, where a man waited for us. He was older, with reddish-gray hair, and he walked with a limp. He looked past his prime. Though he wore a nice suit, he had messy hair and a five o'clock shadow. He spoke with a pointed Brooklyn accent.

"You boys must be Brandon and Noah," he said. "I'm John Tork."

"Yes sir," I said. "It's nice to meet you."

Noah wasn't much for conversing with strangers, he let me do much of the talking.

"Do you have all of your belongings here?" John said.

"Yes."

"Good, let's go," John said.

He walked us to a black Cadillac with pitch black windows. We loaded our stuff in his trunk, which I recall reminding me of a mobster's trunk. It was big enough to hold a body. I sat in the passenger seat with Noah in the back.

"So, where you boys from?" John asked.

"Omaha, Nebraska, born and raised," I answered.

"Nebraska?" John asked skeptically. "What's in Nebraska?"

"Now that we're gone, not much," I joked, trying to break the ice

He let out a little giggle.

"I'm going to take you back to the hotel and let you boys catch up on some sleep today. You'll need it," John said.

124

We were happy to hear that. Though when he got to the hotel, we didn't get much sleep. First thing when we got there, they split us up in separate rooms. All the other people were gone for the day. They'd be returning late that night. We crashed for the day and were woken up around 5 p.m. and taken to John Tork's room. When we arrived, there were two tall, beefy guys wearing suits. They looked like body builders. They didn't say anything to us, only opened the door when we got there. Tork was sitting at a desk in a large hotel room. It must've been the biggest room available at the hotel. It was like a scene out of *Casino*. Stacks of dollar bills surrounded John on his desk. These stacks piled three feet high in various denominations, $1, $5, $10 and $20s. I had never seen that much money at one time. It was intimidating. John welcomed us in and had us sit down at a side table.

"Here, boys," he said. "We've got some paperwork for you to fill out. Lois get your ass in here. We've got two new sign-ups. I need that fucking paperwork."

"I'm coming, calm your britches!" she said to him.

"I'm calm, but we ain't got all day. Business to do, money to make," he said.

"You boys are set to make a bunch of money, you see?" He pointed to all the money at the desk. "You make sales and you make money with each sale. It's easy. We give you cash every day for food. If you need anything else, shoes, clothes, you let me know."

To us it sounded like a sweet deal.

"Here you boys go. Fill these out, if you have any questions let me know," Lois said.

As we were filling out the paperwork, John was yelling at his sales team leads about various things.

"Goddamn it, Freddy, you need to be keeping up, quotas are important around here, you fucking know that," he said.

125

Noah and I were growing uneasy, but we continued to read the legalese and fill out the document with our personal information.

"Lois, get me some fucking lemonade," he snapped.

"I'll get it in a minute," she said, stuffing papers in a filing cabinet.

"Hurry the fuck up, I'm thirsty," he said.

"Here's how it works boys," John said. "You will be put into different teams. We've got about 50 salesmen, and we split into 6 groups. On each team there's a leader who works with salesmen and answers directly to me. You're to follow their orders. You do that and we're good. Every day you'll come down for our morning meeting, and afterwards you'll set off in your groups to different suburbs and towns around the area."

Lois arrived with the lemonade, in a tall plastic cup. John picked it up and took a big swig, setting the cup down next to one of the stacks of money, spilling a little on the table.

"Your leader will drop you off and you'll have all day to make sales," John said. "You go door-to-door and make your pitch – we sell magazines – and if they bite, you close the sale. If they don't, you thank them and move on. You'll have a daily quota. It's important you hit your quota. Every team has a quota, and we compete with each other. If you do well, you'll make a shit ton of money boys."

I interrupted him.

"How much is our quota?" I asked.

"You'll start at 5," John said, "But it will grow and change depending on your last day."

"How much do we make for each sale?" I asked.

"You're getting to the important stuff," John said. "I can see you're sharp, I like that. "You make $30 for each sale," John said. "When you get back each night, you come to me, you turn in your sales, we mark

126

the books to see how you're doing, and we pay you for the next day. We keep the money from your sales on your books. We're like your bank. And at the end of the year we go to a big vacation. Last year it was Hawaii, this year we think we're going to do a cruise along Alaska."

I didn't like the thought of other people holding my money, but figured it was normal.

"You said you're like a bank," I said. "Can we withdraw money when we need it?"

"I will get you whatever you need," John said. "But we've had issues in the past with people willy-nilly taking cash out and blowing it, so we're careful. But like I said, if you need something you just ask."

There were red flags, but we were onboard, at the very least for two weeks.

"And at the end of two weeks, if this isn't for us, you'll pay our way home?"

"Yes," he said. "If you don't like it here, we'll send you home."

We finished our paperwork and left to meet our group leaders.

***

My group leader's name was Philemon. He was brash and reckless as well as loud.

"Brandon!!" Philemon said. "You're my guy. I'm counting on you to be a homerun and you're going to be a knockout for us. You hear me, give me some!"

He put his fist out looking for confirmation. I wasn't as sure as he was, but I was willing to try. I gave him a fist bump.

"You're on our squad now!" he said. "We've got the best fucking squad. We've got the best salesmen and you're gonna help us. Now get outta here, go have some fun. I'll see you tomorrow morning, bright and early."

After leaving Philemon's room, I met my roommate.

"Hey man, I'm Jeremy," he said. "Where you from?"

"I'm Brandon, it's nice to meet you," I said. "I'm from Omaha, Nebraska. How about you?"

"St. Louis," he said.

"You'll like this group a lot, we work hard but we have fun, too. Do you party?"

"What do you mean?" I asked.

"Do you smoke…like weed or drink or do coke or anything?" he asked.

"No," I said.

"Oh," he said clearly hoping for a different answer. "Are you cool with it?"

"Yeah, I don't care, I just don't drink or do drugs," I said.

"Most people here do a lot of drugs," he said.

He wasn't lying. Later that night I walked from my hotel room to Noah's to see how he was doing. There were about 50 people in the entire group, and we took a large block of rooms. I passed 10 different rooms on my walk to Noah's room, all with outdoor entrances. Most of the doors were wide open. They all belonged to people from the group. In one room there was a guy playing an X-box. This was 2004 after all. In another room, there were a couple guys partying with a few girls with music blaring. A third room had two dudes doing coke off the bathroom counter and a fourth had a guy, who was bald, jamming out to metal

128

music while drinking. Every room had drugs or alcohol present. I got to Noah's room and he looked like a ghost.

"Hey man, what's up?" I asked.

"Not much, people doing coke and drinking, like its normal," he said sarcastically.

"We got two weeks man, we got this," I said to reassure him.

We both had our doubts about whether this would work, but we got ourselves into this mess. We were eighteen and we were going to see ourselves through to the end. Having no safety nets, no parents to call to save us, we had no choice.

Chapter 19 – Hard Lessons

Back at my room in the hotel, I got ready for bed. I was still exhausted and fell asleep rather quickly. I woke up in the middle of the night to my roommate having intercourse in the bed next to me with his girlfriend. I wasn't offended, but it was gross.

The next day at the group meeting, things went from weird to tense. John Tork walked to the front of the room and everyone got quiet.

"Alright, folks," he said looking down at his papers. "We've got five of our teammates that need a little extra push today. Yesterday Dylan, Bree and Darius had zero sales."

People in the room started booing. A couple people started picking on one guy.

"No sales? You suck Dylan!" someone close to the guy yelled.

"Get some sales pussy! Are you even trying?"

John Tork motioned the crowd down.

"We don't have much time," John said. "We need you all to hit your quotas. If you miss your quotas, you owe us money. That's how this works, guys. You know that."

"Dylan, you're reaching the end of your rope my friend," John said. "We're going to have to cut the cord soon if you don't make quota. You owe us almost $2,000 as it is."

John went over a few other notes, about where the groups would be going for the day, and celebrating our arrival. Afterwards we broke into our small groups. My group, led by Philemon, had about eight people, from all walks of life. My roommate was in there, along with his girlfriend, another quiet girl who looked physically depressed – I later found out she was addicted to meth.

We drove all the way out to Lancaster, a small Dutch suburb with a median income more than double the national average. Philemon drove the big 9-passenger van. It had burn holes in the seats from cigarettes, dirty, smudged up windows and it smelled like cheap weed. After we all climbed in and headed out, the other salesmen passed two hand-rolled joints back and forth while Philemon drove like a madman. He swerved in and out of traffic on the highway. I sat on the front row seats and could see the speedometer climb north of 85 mph. The speed limit was 55. I tried to stay cool as everyone else was, but I was scared to death. To add to the craziness, Philemon yelled and yipped as we drove past people on the road.

"Get the fuck out of here, you Dutch fuckers!" he screamed, passing them on the highway. "This is our country!"

They dropped me off along a busy street with the guy who I was to shadow for the first day. His name was Davie. He was shorter, and he seemed like a good kid, compared to the others. When we got out of the bus, he shot me straight.

"I've got 10 for my quota today, so just sit back and watch me," he said. "Take mental notes and pick up what you can. We will talk about stuff after each stop. Okay?"

"Sounds good," I said.

At the first stop, I realized that I wasn't in Nebraska anymore. The house was a large white two-story with a two-car garage. We knocked once and a woman, who was about 35 answered the door.

"Can I help you?" she said puzzled.

"Yeah, my name is Dan," Davie said lying to the woman. "I live over on Bradley Street, I'm a junior at Penn State and we're trying to raise money for a trip to England. We're selling magazine subscriptions."

"We're not interested," she said.

"I'm only three subscriptions short from making my goal," he said. "Then I'll be able to stay the entire summer over in England for a study program for the education program I'm a part of."

"We don't need any magazines," she said. "My husband has enough."

"That's okay," he said. "You can donate them to children's shelters or to the troops over in Iraq. Or you can also just make a donation."

"Oh really?" she said. "Yeah we don't need any more magazines. But I'll donate one to the troops. My nephew is over in Iraq."

"Great!" he said. "They need all the support they can get. Here is a list of magazines available."

He handed her a booklet showing magazines, everything from *Sports Illustrated*, to *People*, to Oprah's magazine.

"How much for a yearly subscription?" she asked.

"$40 for one year, $60 for two years," he said.

"I'll take one *Sports Illustrated* and send it to the troops," she said. "I'm glad to be helping you and the troops at the same time."

"Can I pay by check?" the woman asked.

"Yes, but cash is preferable," Davie said.

"I don't have cash but can get you a check," she said.

"That works just fine."

After completing the transaction and leaving the first house, Dylan looked over to me.

"Checks fucking suck," he said. "We get less money for checks on the sale and we get yelled at for not getting cash. John Tork has to pay processing fees for them."

"Why did you lie about who you were, where you were from?" I asked.

"It's the name of the game," he said. "We need sales. We get them any and every way we can."

"How do we send the magazines to children's shelters or to the troops?" I asked.

"We don't," he said. "It's a lie. Like I said, we get the cash how we can, anyway possible."

It shook me when I realized exactly how this game worked. These people, John Tork and the other "leaders" were preying on weak kids who came from broken homes. It took me many years to realize I was one of them too. I wasn't looking at this from the outside. I was in the middle of it. All these kids, Noah and I included, were vulnerable. Many of us had no homes to return to.

Our next stop was a retirement community.

"This place is a gold mine," Dylan said. "Anytime you can get an elderly person, you're already three-steps ahead of a normal sale."

We knocked on the first door. Dylan changed his whole way of trying to make sales.

"Hi, my name is Billy," Dylan said. "I live over off Sky View Lane, just a few blocks over."

"It's nice to meet you," an old woman said after opening the door.

"My little 10-year-old brother Mikey is very sick. He's got Leukemia, he's been fighting for his life since he was 6-years-old. The cancer went away many times, but it's back again...and he's not doing well. Our doctor's expenses have been piling up for months and my mom is unsure we'll have enough to pay them off. I'm walking the community. This is my cousin Jake."

He pointed to me.

"Anything you have to offer will help," Dylan said. "Please...Mikey needs help."

"Oh, that sounds terrible, honey," the woman said. "I'm so very sorry to hear that. I don't have much but hang out one second."

She left the door open and walked out of sight into a back room. She came back after a few moments.

"Here you go, sweetheart," she said, handing over a 20 dollar bill. "It's not much, but I hope it helps. God bless you. I'll be praying for your brother Mikey."

"Thank you so much," Dylan said. "This is a blessing. God bless you too."

I was flummoxed, my stomach was turning. I didn't speak up or say anything. I let it happen. We went to other doors and asked other elderly people for money. We left the community that day with several hundred dollars'-worth of "sales" in tow. Another trick Dylan used was telling people that if they bought a subscription with a check, they could cancel the check within 48 hours. It would count as a sale for him and *not* charge the buyer. It was a complete lie. He was able to make at least one sale a day this way, he told me.

I came to find these kids were fully incased in this lifestyle. Some had been there for five years. It was hard for me to wrap my head around. They were hardened to any wrongs they committed. They felt nothing when lying to people's faces and stealing their money. We worked 14-hours that day and got picked up where we were dropped off that morning. The groups worked 6-days-a-week, with Sunday off.

***

That next morning, at the main meeting, John Tork called Dylan's name again and made him come to the front of the room.

"Yesterday, again, Dylan got no sales," he said as the group started booing. "This motherfucker...this leech...is taking from you – from our family – and he's not contributing anything back."

People began throwing things at Dylan as he stood there at the front of the room. Water bottles, empty boxes of Pop Tarts, balled-up paper balls and pens.

"Dylan, this is your last shot," John Tork said. "Today is the day. You come back with no sales and you're a goner."

John clenched his teeth, hitting Dylan in the back of the head.

"Get the fuck out of my sight," John Tork said. "I don't want to look at you anymore."

The crowd cheered. In that moment it was all starting to come together. These people, these kids did whatever John Tork and their groups leaders wanted. And they used these kids in any and every way possible. John Tork created the rules and he made them up as he went.

"Joe, are those fucking flip flops?" John asked a boy from the audience.

"Yeah," Joe said with his head down.

"That's a $5 dollar fine," he said. "We're taking that off your books.

There were also fines for being late, talking up when not spoken to and many other arbitrary offenses John Tork didn't like in the moment.

Every night when we turned in our sales, John Tork gave us $20 cash for the next day. It was meant to feed us and cover clothes, deodorant and toothpaste. After talking with Dylan, I realized we were supposed to pay for everything. When John Tork told me he would get us clothes and whatever we needed, he wasn't lying, but that debt was put

135

on our books. I found out many people were "in the red," that they didn't have any money saved. You had to sell very well to ever break even. Something like 18 or 20 sales a day.

That next day I was on my own. They dropped me off in a suburb of Harrisburg, PA. I walked for about six hours, knocking on doors and trying to make sales. I had no luck. People were wary of me; my stories were bad. I told the truth when selling, that I was just selling magazines. No one took the bait. I went to a corner store for lunch and ate a hot dog and a bag of chips with a soda. I walked for another eight hours after that. We got picked up from the same spot we were dropped off that morning. It was dark, my legs ached, and my back hurt.

I went to see John Tork after the day and though he was not happy with me, he wasn't yelling. He tried to be somewhat encouraging.

"The best thing you can do is clean up," he said. "Try to look like a normal neighborhood kid. Know your surroundings, know the streets you're on, and find the lie that they bite on. If you believe what you're saying, they'll believe it too."

He gave me $20 for the next day.

"These two days are your only free days," he said. "Tomorrow, I'm expecting you to have four sales. It's not much. I believe in you. Don't make me regret it."

I felt a pinch inside my chest. I knew this wasn't for me.

That night at the hotel I tried to sleep, but the noise in the room next to mine was too much. The music blasted as loud as possible, it seemed. Under the music I could hear yelling, screaming, and later, cries for help. My roommate was gone. I got up to the window and opened it enough to hear more what was going on. As I did, a girl burst out of the next door over half naked. She was stumbling and clearly drunk or high. She ran past my door to her room, slamming the door. The music next door shut off and three guys left after her. They had their shirts off and two had visible scratches on them. They laughed and joked with each

136

other, high fiving. I can only imagine what happened in that room that night. From the stories Dylan told me, a lot of the people had group sex sessions together. This was different. It seemed like rape. I called the cops and told the dispatcher that I thought someone was being raped in the room next to mine. I peeked and found the room number. I didn't tell them who I was, and I hung up. Police showed up about 20 minutes later and asked several of the people outside questions. I watched from the crack in the window. The girl spoke with them. I assume nothing happened, because they left and the girl went back to her room. Soon after I finally went to bed.

***

Bright and early the next day, before the meeting, I walked over to Noah's room to see how he was doing. I knocked on his door and he answered right away, coming outside like he was waiting for me. Before I could say anything, he cut in.

"Dude, I can't do this anymore," he said. "I feel like I've sold my soul."

"I know. This is crazy," I said. "They were stealing money from old people during my first day at a retirement community. I got yelled at by Tork for getting no sales. How'd you do yesterday?"

"I didn't sell anything, but I didn't try," he said. "I walked around town, then went to the woods and enjoyed nature. I can't do it. I'm leaving."

"Okay, let's leave after two weeks," I said.

"I can't do it," he said. "I can't wait two weeks. I'm leaving today."

I wasn't going to let Noah leave alone and I didn't want to be there by myself. So, in the few moments, realization hit me. We we're leaving.

"Okay," I said. "Let's go tell John Tork."

Before we told Tork, we told our groups individually. They tried to talk us out of it. They told us we were just homesick. That as we became better salesmen, we'd like it better with the group if we stayed longer. We explained we were Midwestern boys who were raised in the church, this wasn't the life for us. While that was true, it had more to do with them being an evil, cult-like cluster of thieves. After I told my group, I had to tell Philemon, our group leader. He wasn't happy, and he flipped a switch from being my friend to saying, "To hell with you then, bye!"

After telling our groups and group leaders, Noah and I walked to John Tork's hotel room. The two bodyguards knocked on the door.

"Enter," Tork said.

We walked in sheepishly. John knew what was going on and looked pissed. I tried to explain that this wasn't for us, that we wanted to go home. I tried to thank him for his hospitality, but he cut me off.

"The fuck with your thank yous! I wouldn't give two squirts of piss to care about your thank yous. You signed a contract, and you failed to live it out. If you want out, then FUCKING LEAVE!"

"Aren't you going to send us home, with tickets for a Greyhound?"

He laughed, sitting up in his chair.

"We're not paying for shit," he said. "You didn't make it two weeks. The way I see it, you owe us for the hotel stay for three nights and the money we loaned you. You want to leave? You want to go home? Good. Get the fuck out of here. You're not getting a cent. You can fucking starve."

138

We said okay and left the room. We thought it best not to upset a man sitting at a large desk covered with stacks of cash guarded by men strapped with firearms. We just wanted out and we got it.

Luckily, we had packed everything we owned into our bags and had it with us, because I had the feeling we wouldn't be able to get our things, had we left them in our rooms.

Years later, we later found out that Tork and his cronies skirted state and federal employment laws which allowed them to not have to pay us any minimum or hourly wage because they considered us independent contractors and not actual employees. It was their wild game of human trafficking.

After leaving Tork's office, we went to the hotel lobby and used the courtesy computer. I used Xanga, to make a social media post letting people know we were coming home. Then Noah and I counted our money. I had spent most of the allotted money given to me on food. Noah, however, saved all his. Thank God. We pooled funds, which meant I added my five dollars to his fifty. We went to the lobby to use the payphones. We knew calling our parents and family wouldn't matter. They had no means to get us and we both knew they'd laugh in our faces with "I told you so's." We were stranded and on our own. But, we didn't care. We escaped what could've been much worse.

I asked Noah who to call. He thought it was a good idea to call "K-Love," a Christian radio station with a national audience, mostly because Noah had the phone number memorized. I put change in the pay phone and dialed the number.

"Thanks for calling K-Love," the person said. "Can I pray for you to accept the Lord today?"

"Actually, I'm already saved," I said. "I'm in a bind..."

I explained everything from being kicked out from Vinnie's house to John Tork and the evil cult-like salespeople. She told me there was nothing she could do but asked to pray for me. She also said she could give me a list of local churches to call for help. I wrote down three she gave me, thanked her and hung up.

Luckily it was Sunday morning, so churches were in service. I called the first on the list and a woman answered. I told me story, explained that it sounded farfetched, but that we needed help. She set the phone down, came back after a few minutes and told us to come to their church. Thank God, I thought. I called a taxi service who picked us up and we went to the church. It was about a 20-minute drive.

Noah and I arrived at the church, walked up with all our belongings and met with the woman I spoke with on the phone. I explained our trouble, that we needed $140 to go home, two tickets to Omaha. Noah and I showed them our IDs and our tickets from Omaha to Philly. They were having a luncheon after church. The woman heard our story and invited us to sit down and eat some food. We thanked her and ate.

There were sub sandwiches, pasta salad and a myriad of sides. We ate our fill. As we were eating and discussing how crazy this experience had been, we noticed the woman was talking with a group of men who kept looking over our shoulders. I thought to myself that we were all Christians, that these people were bound to help us. That's what the tribe does! They'd at least let us stay with them and do some yard work/odd jobs to earn the money. We didn't care. Two of the men walked over to us.

"Hey once you finish up eating," he said. "We're going to have you come with us. We're going to take you to the Open Door Mission."

I was angry. We didn't need a ride to the Open Door Mission. We could walk there. We needed a ride home. But we agreed. After the meal we got into the car and as we drove, I'll never forget what the guy said to us.

"I bet you've never met a Youth Pastor who listened to AC/DC, huh?" he asked.

"I've never met a Youth pastor who completely missed the mission of Christ and helping those in need, right in front of him," I thought to myself.

They dropped us off and wished us well. That was it. I couldn't be angry. Technically, they owed us nothing. But it was frustrating to think that Christians could act this way with two people who needed help.

The Open Door Mission's entryway was in the alley. There was a sign on the door that read: OPENS AT 4PM, BEDS ARE FIRST COME, FIRST SERVED.

It was about 12 p.m. and Noah and I sat on the stoop near the doorway. Two homeless men smoked cigarettes and talked about the Eagles football game that day. Sitting in the alley, I lost hope. No one was going to save us. Looking the two men smoking, I felt like Noah and I were looking at our futures had we not left the mission.

Noah looked over to me.

"Dude, I'm not staying here," he said. "I'd rather die on the streets walking than stay here."

Noah had spent a few years as a kid living in an Open Door Mission with his family. His dad and mom were married in the ODM in Omaha in 1989. I attended the wedding. I never lived in one, but I ate meals there as a kid.

We decided our best bet would be to leave – to hitch hike home. So, we left. Luckily, I had a map of the city I'd gotten from the hotel. I pulled it out and figured we needed to walk west to the Interstate. From there, we could find a place to sleep for the night near the road. We started walking. We passed a bunch of downtown shops and offices. We even passed the first real punk rock concert I've ever seen with a guy in the crowd wearing a leather jacket and a spiky Mohawk, about 10 inches off his head. The music was terrible. That's how I knew it was real punk rock.

After about 30 minutes of walking I realized we were walking east, not west. Noah laughed at me in desperation, saying if we died it was my fault. He said he felt like we were the Donner party, but instead of being in the wilderness, we were in one of the poorest, densest areas of Philly. We knew we needed a break. So, we stopped at a Catholic Church and sat down on the concrete steps in front of the cathedral. Noah went to a corner shop nearby to buy us a couple drinks. He came back with some sodas and we drank our fill. Our bags got to be too much to carry. I thought, what better place to leave a bunch of clothes and shoes that we didn't need any more than a Catholic Church? It made sense at the time. We left more than half of the clothes we had on the front steps of the gigantic cathedral.

We set off again, this time, in the right direction.

"Noah, can you believe it?" I asked, wanting to cry, but only able to laugh at our stupidity and predicament. "We have no one to call, and nothing to do but count on ourselves to get home. What are we going to do?"

"Try not to die," he said half-joking.

After about another 30 more minutes of walking, I noticed a nice Lexus SUV parked on the street outside of an attorney's office. It was a bad area of town. The buildings were all connected. Unlike standalone buildings in Nebraska, on the east coast, everything was very close together. As we were passing the attorney's office, I notice a nicely dressed middle-aged woman and her daughter walking out of the building towards the Lexus. I turned to Noah and said:

"Watch this."

I approached the woman and her daughter.

"You wouldn't happen to have $140 we could have for two tickets home, would you?" I said smiling, leading into the long spiel about who we were, where we were from, and our story as magazine salesmen.

We pulled our wallets out and showed her our Nebraska State IDs, showed her our original tickets from Omaha to Philly, and even showed her a pamphlet we received from church that I had in my wallet with our church's address in Omaha. She seemed worried and questioned our story. We explained we weren't lying, showed her all the money we had, and proved how much the original tickets were.

"I don't normally do this," she said. "I would never help some stranger on the street, but something is telling me to help you."

Whatever it was, I was hoping she would listen to that voice. She paused, looking us up and down.

"I'm going to need to pat you down and check your pockets before I let you in my car," she said.

"Do what you need," I said.

I didn't care what she wanted proof of, or reassurance of, I just wanted to go home. She checked our things, bags, pockets, and patted us down, looking for weapons and the like. After patting us down, I could sense her comfort knowing we weren't bad people.

"Okay, get in and let's go," she said.

I thought, 'there are good people left in this world.' As we approached the Greyhound station I got giddy with childish exuberance. We were going home.

"I don't know if you believe in God or not, but I want you to know that I feel like there is something bigger at work here," I said.

"Actually, I'm Jewish," she said.

We all had a good laugh. We got out of her car and went to the station. She ordered two tickets to Omaha, Nebraska, from the ticket window, took the money we had and paid for the rest. Then she handed us the tickets. Coincidentally enough, our bus was arriving as we were ordering. We gave our bags to the driver to throw underneath the bus, turning to the woman.

"Thank you so much!" I said. "Can I give you a hug?"

She obliged.

"Do you need money for food?" she said. "I don't want you two to starve; it's a long drive."

She turned from questioning our intent when she met us to a loving, caring mother in 20 minutes flat. She could've paid for our tickets, said "That's enough," and let us go on our way, but she wanted to know we would not go hungry. I've never felt better about humanity than I did in those few moments. She gave us $20, hugged us and wished us the best. She watched us get on the bus, she and her daughter waving at us as the bus departed.

Noah and I, sitting on the bus, couldn't do anything but laugh back and forth for the next hour. It was the longest week of our lives. These dark times challenged us like nothing had up to that point. But nothing felt better than two days later driving over the Iowa-Nebraska border and seeing the Omaha downtown skyline at dusk. I felt as though, with all we had been through over the past several days, we could walk home from the downtown Omaha Greyhound station. We were home.

Chapter 20 – Taking The Blame

When grandpa died in July of 2000, the family was broken. The great tree had fallen and the seeds scattered. 14-year-old me thought I could hold the family together. I had no idea of how the deaths of patriarchs and matriarchs impacted family structures. My grandma got left in the aftermath. Grandpa died on their 59th wedding anniversary and she took his death hard, but she was a strong woman. I only saw her crying the day of his death, and never again after that.

During Christmas break in 2000, I spent the entire week at grandma's house. I took three city buses to get there, and I stole $20 in food stamps from my mom. I used the funds to walk to the bread store and buy goodies for Grandma and me.

Spending time at grandpa's house was always a great escape. It was restorative. The best memories I had were all there. After Grandpa died, I still loved going over. But there was a huge hole in the place. I spent a lot of time in the attic, grandpa's old room. He wasn't there, but I could feel him. I was always waiting for grandpa to come walking down the stairs, whistling or singing opera like he always used to. The house was like our family, hollow without him.

Grandpa always gave us everything we wanted. Grandma made us earn it. Don't get me wrong, I loved grandma and I knew she loved me deeply, but I gravitated, like many in the family, to grandpa. After he passed, I did all I could to enjoy grandma's company. Partially to better grasp who grandpa was. Who in this world knew him better than his wife of six decades? Part of me also felt that I owed it to her, because I wasn't as close to her as grandpa.

***

Grandma always stayed up late, usually until 3 or 4 a.m. Then she'd wake up around 11 a.m. or noon, just in time to watch her soap operas. *All My Children*, *One Life to Live* and *General Hospital* were her favorites. She'd watched them since they started, some in the 1960s. She always sat in the kitchen. Her chair was padded with added cushions, and the arms had cushions made from hand towels and rubber bands. Everything grandma used had a spot, and if you needed something like Carmex lip balm or cough drops, she fetched them from little nooks in the large stacks of newspapers on her table. She could retrieve anything in moments. She had a complex system. You didn't mess around. She *knew* when you took something or misplaced something.

"Brandon James!" she yelled at me from the kitchen with a hint of vibrato. "What have you done with my Carmex?"

I can still hear her voice. Like grandpa's it's written on my heart.

I remember countless days after grandpa died, grandma and I would sit in the kitchen watching soap operas and talking about grandpa. I asked her everything. I wanted to know everything I could: what grandpa was like as a young man, what it was like being married to him. I wanted to know about when he was in the service in Arkansas before the babies and before the War. When he was stationed in Arizona and Alaska after the kids were born in the '50s, what was it like living with him on post? Were dad's kids grandpa's favorites? How was he different as a parent and grandfather? What happened the morning grandpa died, how did she find him? Did he believe in God?

I asked her about my dad, too. I was curious about his upbringing and his formative years. She went to her deathbed believing that dad was innocent. Even after I told her everything that happened the night he pushed Kim down the stairs, she believed it was an accident. I think it was because she knew she wouldn't be able to see him again in her life – he

146

would be in prison when she died. I tried to persuade her he did it intentionally. He meant to hurt Kim, but he didn't want to kill her. She could not be convinced. I was dismayed. This was her son, though. She knew his shortcomings and protected him from day one. In her eyes, he was a dipstick, but he was her dipstick.

I spent most of my time at grandma's house, post grandpa's death, in the living room. I'd watch sports, music videos, anything I could find. I also started writing recaps of sporting events and reading them to grandma. She was my first audience.

***

In 2004, after graduating, I planned to move to El Paso, Texas with friends. I decided not to move about two days before we left. Grandma talked me out of it. She never spelled it out, but I could tell if I left she'd have been heartbroken. When I went to Philadelphia, she was the first to tell me how stupid it was for me to leave. She didn't want me to go, but I had nowhere else. I wasn't going to ask to live with her. It didn't seem right asking her to care for me. I had to see the world, and what it offered on my own, for myself.

I called her every single day. Sometimes five or six times a day. I'd update her on everything going on in my life from the latest girl I was seeing or had a crush on to how dad was doing in prison since he also called her a lot. I'd ask about the latest gossip in the family, too. We talked Husker football and she'd give me updates on *General Hospital*. We talked about everything under the sun. Grandma also chatted about my mother and stepdad – she still thought they were "trash," years after her and dad's divorce. She told me a lot about how bad of a mother my mom was, specifically the neglect she showed as a young mother when I was a baby.

In early April 2006, I called grandma. The phone rang many times, way more than normal. She finally answered.

"Hey Grandma, what's up? It's Brandon," I said.

"I'm just lying down," she said, her speech somewhere slurred. "I'm not feeling well."

"Are you okay?" I asked. "Do you need to go see a doctor?"

"No," she said. "I've just got a little bug."

"Are you drinking fluids, water?" I asked

"Plenty of them," she said.

I didn't want to bother her. I wanted her to rest.

"Okay, I'll let you go. I love you, grams," I said.

"Love you too," she said.

I found out several days later at work that she wasn't doing well. My aunt had taken her to the hospital. The doctor said she had the worst case of pneumonia he had ever seen. Both her lungs were completely filled with fluids. She wasn't taking in oxygen, and she was hallucinating on carbon dioxide. They put her on meds to help quell the infection, and it worked. Within a few days she was awake, chewing on pieces of ice and writing on a notepad to communicate. My aunt said she woke up one day in the hospital and saw most of her family standing around her laughing and telling stories.

The next day the infection came roaring back and the doctors couldn't stop it – they couldn't save her. She died. I got a call at work that day that I needed to rush to the hospital to see her before she passed. She was unconscious, but people were saying their goodbyes.

My aunt Leona gave me a ride to Emmanuel Hospital in Omaha. Grandma was already dead. People in the room stood around her body, everyone crying. She didn't look like grandma. Her body was experiencing what is called Alger Mortis, where the body cools to room temperature. The skin around her face had shrunk and her mouth was agape. It looked very sad. I didn't cry that day though. I was the last to leave the room. I went to her and gave her a kiss on her forehead, and she smelled just like the grandma I always remembered. I whispered in her ear.

"I love you, gramma," I said. "I promise to be a good boy."

She always told me when I left the house that she loved me and to "be a good boy."

I wanted her to know that I always would be.

On the day of her funeral, I wrote a long, heartfelt speech about how everyone loved grandpa, and how after he passed I got to know her better. My aunt brought the birthday card that grandma bought me that year, just a few weeks before. I hadn't been by to get it from her yet. I opened it in real time, standing at the podium.

She always bought us lots presents and the cards always seemed to be throwaways, at least when you're a kid. Your parents tend to make you read them to understand there was love behind this present. A person gave something *to you* and you should understand their expression of love. Grandma always signed the cards the same way: "All Our Love, Grandpa and Grandma McD." As I opened this card, I read the message. At the end she wrote:

"All My Love, Always, Grandma McD"

I held it together for the most part before that, but I broke down at that point.

I'll never forget our time together, even more so than my time with Grandpa. He was encased in marble to me – untouchable – perfect from the eyes of small Brandon. Grandma and I had a relationship that no one else in the family got. I got to know her in her final years after she raised kids and grandkids and after she lived a full life and lost her best friend. I'm grateful for my time with her, the stories she shared, the love she gave and the closeness I got to experience with her.

Grandpa's guidance shaped me. Grandma's hardiness and support pushed me. He was lionized in my young mind when he died. I was able to take those shared life lessons and adopt them. I picked up Dad's ability to push people's buttons in an argument. I've wanted to succeed because it would make grandpa proud. Uncle Vinnie's general "I'll do it my way," attitude is ingrained in me. With grandma, it's the capacity to withstand life's slow crawl to inevitable annihilation that I've taken. There was no one more resilient than her. She was strong to the end.

***

I didn't visit dad much throughout his time in prison. He was sentenced to 18 to 20 years in prison for manslaughter. I did visit him periodically from about 2001 to 2002. My Aunt Mary and her husband Dan were nice enough to give us rides to see him. My mother had neither the means nor the will to get us to where he was held in Tecumseh, Nebraska, about 70 miles away. Grandma asked my aunt to drive us and she did, even after I stopped going. Brittney stopped going too, eventually. Mary and Dan still took my youngest sister. They continued to do this even after my grandma died.

When we'd visit dad in prison, we were only allowed a hug at the start and finish of the visit. We'd chat, eat vending machine food and talk about our lives. Dad always spoke about being better, doing better and making a difference when he got out. It sounded to 15- and 16-year-old Brandon like he was finally understanding what he did. He was going to be try to be a changed man. I had faith for the future. How could you not want better than being locked up? I thought.

Sometime in 2002 I received a letter from dad. He sent me many letters throughout his time in prison. This one was different. At the top of the page, above the "Dear Brandon," it read:

ABANDON BRANDON!!!

He went in on me, counting the reasons why it was my fault he got caught and locked up. He blamed me for turning him into the police saying:

"The plan was solid. All you had to do was keep the message straight. You betrayed me and failed me. I'm in here because of you!"

As much as I want to say that he was wrong, I felt what he said was true. He continued:

"I didn't get to see my father at his funeral because of you. I never got to say goodbye to him, you took that from me. I'll never be able to hug my mother again or see her face and it's your fault. I raised you right and all you did was shit on me. You have to live with that for the rest of your life. Grandpa died knowing this!"

I was broken. I internalized that pain – in my mind truth – for many, many years. I'm still unpacking the trauma and reminding myself it is okay. To this day, I feel like I'm paying for both his sins to society and for my own. He knew I would. Compared to all the beatings, verbal lashings, sexual abuse and emotional weight he put on me, this was worse. It felt heavier. I'm not sure why he punished me like this, but it worked – it had long-term effects that I'm still wading through. This book helped in that process, spilling the memories and feelings onto paper reminded me how far I've come as a man.

***

Dad blamed a terrible lawyer for getting him to plead no contest and skip a trial. At no time did he take the blame. He never had to in his life and he didn't start even after the most heinous crime one can commit: taking a life.

He was granted parole in May 2009 after ten years in prison because of good behavior. He moved immediately to my Aunt Mary's house. He lived there for free. In the meantime, he was given money from the sale of my grandfather and grandmother's house after they passed. They split it evenly among their kids. After court and lawyer fees he got somewhere around $10,000. What man or woman coming out of jail has that type of nest egg?

He squandered that cash within months. Aunt Mary gave him Grandpa's green GM truck that I had my last ride in with him in before he died. Dad's first stop was Best Buy on 76th and Dodge in Omaha – he spent $800 on a tricked out stereo system. It was a nice one, but as always, he lacked foresight.

Before he got out of jail, he started talking to my half-brother's mother Annabelle. She was bad news and they went off like a fireworks display in a wooden shed. They burned fast and furious, ruining everything in sight. He moved in with Annabelle and things went even further south. He paid all her utility bills and debt that hadn't been paid in months. He also fueled her cigarettes and case a day Coca Cola habits. His funds were dwindling fast.

Because it only made sense, they got married in her house on a summer day two months after he was released. It was a poorly planned, low-quality wedding. Everyone in attendance, including the rent-by-the-hour minister, knew this would fail. They held the ceremony in her messy living-room. I oversaw hitting play on the music: Firehouse's *Love of a Lifetime.*

The marriage didn't last a month.

Annabelle kicked him out of her house and I thought he learned from his mistakes because he didn't stalk her. He did drive by her house a ton, but for him, that was an improvement. He was flat broke. He'd failed to save any of the money or secure a place to live. He was a felon and he had his nose in the air – he was above lowly fast food work, which is quintessential dad. He never had to work for anything and he was gifted more than $10,000 *after* going to prison, yet he had nothing to show for it save for a failed marriage and a car stereo. He'd learned nothing from 50 years of his mistakes and had nothing worthwhile in his life to show for it.

My sister Brittney and I lived in a house on North 40th Ave between Bedford and Spencer in North Omaha. I was 23 and Brittney was 22. We let dad move in with us for free, food included. He slept on the couch. He liked to sleep throughout the day, never trying to get a job, and one day he yelled at Brittany and me for waking him up. He said we were being too loud. We told him flatly that it was our house and he was to deal with our rules or leave. It was as plain as that. He didn't like being pushed around, so he left.

Within weeks he found another woman. He met her in an odd way. He was living with my sister's ex-boyfriend, an odd circumstance already. He met the woman, Amy, because she lived in the same apartment complex. Within weeks they were living together. It also didn't last long. She broke up with him and kicked him out. This time, he wouldn't go away, and he stalked her actively. He caught her along with her new boyfriend at a blood bank in Omaha. He chased their car in his truck, pulling alongside them. He made some threats to both – that he would kill them, chop them up and no one would find them. Amy called the police. He was arrested and charged with two counts of terroristic threats and one count of stalking. The court convicted and sentenced him to two years. He was released in June of 2012, again, on parole. During this stint in jail, I didn't contact him. No calls and no letters.

He got out of jail in time for my wedding which was set for September of that year. I invited him and my mother to come. They sat at the same table, along with my stepdad. During my thank you speech, I thanked my wife's family for helping pay for the wedding. They paid more than half of the costs.

I found out later that dad wasn't happy because I didn't thank him or mom during the wedding. That was planned. What was I going to thank them for? I figured I had thanked them enough through my hard work and showing them that, while I was their son, I was breaking the cycle they tried to stick my sisters and me in.

After the ceremony and during the reception, he took me outside to talk. He gave me some line about being out of jail and doing better for himself. I'd heard it all before, from when we'd visit when I was 15, to when he was released the first time three years before. I was tired of listening to the same old song and dance. He pulled out his wallet and handed me $20.

"There's more where that came from son," he said. "I'll get you the rest of your wedding gift the next time I see you. I've got some good stuff lined up."

A few weeks later he had moved to southeast Missouri to move in with a 70-year-old woman who wined and dined him because she was lonely. He met her on a chatroom online. He had always been good at finding needy, vulnerable people to take advantage of and this was no different. She bought him a PlayStation 3 and he played video games while she worked at a local gas station. Eventually she tired of him, too, kicking him out.

He made his way back to Nebraska in 2014. When he came back, he called me, but I kept ignoring him. He found my work number online and called me. I didn't recognize the number, so I answered. The conversation was short and to the point.

"Boy, when are you going to put all of this stuff behind us so we can move forward?" he said.

"Dad let me cut you off there," I said. "You are a leech. You've done nothing to help yourself or the ones you claim to love – not once in

154

your pitiful life. Everything I've got, everything I've gained, has not been because of your help but *despite* your attempts to derail my life. I want nothing from you, except for you to never try to contact me or my family again. Move on with your life. I have."

With that, I hung up.

Chapter 21 – Finding Yourself

I was on a business trip in Seattle in November 2018 when it all came together. After years of dealing with my past using music and Husker football as therapy, I knew I needed to do something more. I found digging deep, opening memories I haven't thought about in years and spilling it onto paper was the best way to go forward.

In Seattle it hit me, telling the world everything was the best way to understand my trauma and to help others.

In Seattle, I attended a convention for NPR radio hosts. We all came together to discuss best practices, share training sessions, and get pointers from national hosts. One night after the training sessions ended, we went for some dinner and drinks. I was talking with a well-known NPR host. Our conversation turned to our pasts and our childhoods. After hearing my story, this guy, who will remain nameless, said to me:

"Brandon, you've got quite the story, and I've only heard part of it. You should think about putting this to paper and journaling your experiences. You've seriously got a book on your hands."

I'd long thought about the possibility. Sure, I knew I had plenty of material, perhaps enough for several books, but it would take a concerted effort to share my past. Recalling the memories, putting myself in the same mindset as I was as a child – that was the tough thing for me to overcome. Anyone who has met me will tell you that I have no issue telling my story, as I wear my heart on my sleeve. But the idea of telling the world, that was a different monster all together.

When I announced my plan to write the book, I got a lot of great feedback and positive encouragement which reinforced my idea that I was doing something right. People who follow me on social media and have heard nuggets of my story before chimed in on my posts via email and private message to tell me that my story was helping them in their own lives. This solidified my goal.

One place I didn't think I'd get any pushback was my extended family. Sure, I figured my father and mother wouldn't want me to share what happened with anyone. Besides them, though, I thought I'd get encouragement. Boy, was I was wrong. My uncle Dan reached out to me on Facebook asking me not to "air the family's dirty laundry." He said this "wasn't the right time." What is the right time?

In some ways, I'm just an extension of my father to them, just another black eye on the family name. My sisters and I are a reminder of my father's failures. We *are* the family's dirty laundry. We are the dirt to be brushed under the carpet.

As a kid, I felt forgotten about and tossed away by teachers and a foster family that didn't want me. I had a hatred towards the State of Nebraska for putting me in a youth shelter for so long with kids who were there for their own trouble. All of this only exacerbated the chip on my shoulder. It was a time in my life I had to deal with, that I had to overcome. I was never going to have that conversation with dad or mom that made it all better, that solved any of these issues. I had to accept the apologies that I never got.

One thing grandpa McDermott taught me was to be your own man and take your own road. My uncle Vinnie taught me one thing, too, that I live by: Don't worry about burning bridges, just cross the river directly. People can complain about you all they want, but when you do it alone, they are only talking about you. Let them talk. I'm living my best life, unashamed of my upbringing and I won't bury it any longer. I've endured and am proud of the man I've become. I can look myself in the mirror without being mortified at what I see – not many people can say that.

I once had to give a speech at the Omaha Press Club. It was an acceptance speech on behalf of the scholarship winners at the University of Nebraska at Omaha, of which I was one. I decided early in the process of writing the speech I would discuss what I overcame early in my life. I practiced in the small office of a lecturer who taught radio classes at UNO. I read her a draft I had written. She cut me off about a paragraph in.

"Brandon," she said pausing. "Do you really want to be remembered as the boy who was abused in those ways? People might be put off by this speech. It's a scholarship speech. It's supposed to be a positive look at your scholastic achievements. Why not talk about the people who've helped you?"

I was caught off guard by her message. She said more to me in that moment, about who she was, than I ever needed to make a judgement about her as a person. Fact of the matter is, I *am* that boy. He will always live in me. I can't deny it and I won't run from it anymore. She tried to get me to change the speech, to "tone it down," as she put it. I told her I would, then I went against my word. I didn't feel bad about doing it my way. After the speech, there was a line of people 20 deep waiting to shake my hand and thank me for sharing my story. In that moment, I knew I had done the right thing.

In the end, just as I accepted my past, I had to accept my successes in life too. Sometimes that means offending people; sometimes that means being okay with how people see you: as dirty laundry.

Chapter 22 – Giving Thanks

Growing up, I wasn't the easiest person to deal with. I was hard on my teachers and I could be an unbearable child. I carried the chip on my shoulder like a heart on my sleeve. I suppose at some point I confused the chip on my shoulder with the weight of my trauma. Over the years, perhaps those two began to blur into one. It was a large sack of rocks that I carried everywhere with me. When people acted like they didn't see it, I would rub it into their faces. I wanted to scream at the world for everything I didn't understand. It seemed unfair I was dealt this poor hand and had to scratch and claw to survive, while others didn't have to learn the lessons I had to as a youngster.

Some people don't suffer fools. Well I didn't suffer privileged people. I was sure to tell friends if I thought they were privileged. This cost me many friends.

I also reminded people about what I was dealing with. I didn't like to be compared to others, because in my mind I was nothing like any of them. Yet, I always compared myself to those I considered better off. Coming of age, I had to deal with my baggage and learn to make the best out of what life threw at me. More than anything else, I had to grow up and accept who I was, and what I wasn't. I could continue blaming others (like mom and dad, my stepdad and my uncle Vinnie always did) for my circumstances and shortcomings or I could move on and use what happened *to me* for good. To do better and to *be* better. Like Grandma and Grandpa always saw in me and pushed me towards.

The feeling I've gotten while putting this book together is a lot like meeting an old friend. It was like opening a chapter of my life that was dead, it seems like an eternity away. In some ways it is, as it was twenty years ago. Some of that is still inside me.

I'll have to deal and live with that for the rest of my life. It'll always be right under the surface, because it's a part of who I am. This entire process cleansed me, and yet it burdened me. It took me six months to write the first four chapters then about forty days to write the last eighteen. Once I started and cracked open the box of "old me," it just flowed, the memories, the regrets and the growth. Those old wounds opened easily, perhaps too easily.

One thing that has always puzzled me, was anytime I talked about my father's abuse of my mother the consensus was always: she did the right thing in leaving dad. However, when it came to my sisters and me, many people with varying perspectives on my father – some who had never met him – would say "Yes but he's still your father. You need to call him. You need to love him. He's always going to be your dad."

There is a deep seated rule in our society that says we must respect our elders and love our parents. "You'll regret it someday," that's what we're told.

Let me clear this up for you, there will be no regret. I've lived with regret and have tried to help both my parents throughout their lives. I forgave my mother for how she raised us and what she put us through.

I forgave my father for his years of abuse, both to me and the women in his life. I didn't call him to tell him. That wasn't important to me. It was about giving up on my anger about the past. I had to stop blaming how I acted as an adult on what he did to me. I also can't expect for God to forgive me without first forgiving him. This book has taught me that. With all his evil – abusing kids, women, animals, and killing a mother – I still see that lost little boy who is unable to "get it," when I think of him.

I don't see the scary monster I did when I was young. He is a sociopath, preying on women, children and vulnerable people but he isn't the boogeyman. The one thing the boogeyman needs to survive is fear from others.

160

Society tells us we should care for our own. We shouldn't let our parents get old and die alone. No matter what happened, our parents and still our parents. I do not subscribe to this theory.

I won't grieve for mom or dad when they pass. The fact is, I grieved so long *for them* during their lives – my grief is exhausted.

***

I know what it's like to go without dinner, to go without electricity, to live with periods of no heat or air conditioning. Growing up, I stood in lines at local food pantries, waited for free food and accepted donated Christmas presents from families I'd never meet. We lived in roach-infested apartments and houses. When my mother was too lazy, and we ran out of toilet paper, we would use a communal bath towel to wipe the defecation from our behinds. Sometimes this would go on up to a week. It depended on how hard up for money we were and how lazy my mother had gotten. Remembering the dirty towels piled next to the toilet soaked with the family's feces and urine is a stark reminder of my humble upbringing.

Going to school at some point became a cakewalk. I didn't pay attention to the school work itself because I wasn't being pushed or motivated. But what it did afford me was an opportunity to eat and be around teachers who were better examples than my parents. This was a place I could make connections that still mean something to me.

Going to college was a goal of mine after high school, but I had to overcome my hatred for the thought of higher education. I wasn't able to use federal grants (FAFSA) as my dad was in prison and mom never filed taxes. College kids were 'elites' in my mind. As a naïve, idealistic 20-year-old, to me, kids were able to go to college because their parents paid their way. I had to get over myself. It wasn't their fault that their parents cared for them, loved them and did all they could to ensure they succeeded. I needed to overcome my own pity party to see my growth as a person and as a man. I've had three jobs since graduating high school in 2004. I stayed for six years at a company in Omaha working as a department manager and in customer service. I interned at KVNO, a small radio station in Omaha and worked my way up to News Director. It was fulfilling work. I got to speak into a microphone and get paid for it. But more importantly I got to tell other people's stories. I got to share their pain with the community around them. That is a big part of being a storyteller: letting people know they aren't alone. Their feelings aren't exclusive to them.

At 27, I re-took my ACT and enrolled at UNO. At UNO, I made the Dean's List, the Chancellor's List and was awarded four scholarships. I graduated in May of 2020 summa cum laude with a 3.63 GPA. The key was not waiting for others to motivate me, but to use their lack of faith in me to motivate myself.

When I was told I couldn't do something that *something* became the only goal in my mind. From my teachers telling me I would amount to nothing, to the general manager of the radio station I interned at asking what I was doing there.

"We're not feeding the stray cats, are we?" he said to my news director. This was after the news director hired me, an intern with no college experience.

That hit home. I had no value to him, a lowly volunteer intern. I used his lack of faith in me as fuel to do better and make him eat his words.

I had to get over myself, accept my shortcomings and use them to help me succeed. My perceived deficiencies were strengths. While I didn't have strong memories of my parents, I had their terrible track records to remind me that I could do better. As iron sharpens iron, I had been tempered by suffering. I had dealt with so much trauma early on, I felt unbreakable in a way. I had a hard exterior, a big chip on my shoulder and I was ready for anything life could throw at me. When you're born into flames, you can breathe fire.

162

***

My wife didn't want to be a part of this story, but without her, my story is unfinished, and I am incomplete. I met her on August 26th, 2008. Nine years to the day that Kim was killed by my father. I hope you'll forgive the clichés, but my life was shrouded with clouds before she arrived, and she's been my saving grace since we met. She's that and more.

She loves and cares for me, licking my wounds after long days of stressful work or when I wake up from night terrors crying, sweating and gripped with fear. She also challenges me to do better and be the best man I can be.

In many ways, she reminds me a lot of my grandma McDermott. She's as tough a person as I've ever met, and she cares more deeply than anyone I've encountered. After I was baptized into the world of my father by the blood of my mother, she was the healing I needed to solidify the man I became. She was the first real soft rain I ever felt.

I've been blessed beyond measure. She helped me overcome what was expected of me. My parents didn't graduate high school, so when I did, I felt accomplished. When I had a full-time job with benefits and paid time off, something my parents never had, I believed I had achieved something grand. Lindsay, my wife, pushed me to do better and to be better. She is the one who convinced me to go to college and her persistence is what kept my focus on the straight and narrow during the process. Neither of my parents owned a home. In 2018, Lindsay and I bought our first house in Lincoln. The sky is the limit, not because of how great I am, but because of how great she is.

***

I knew my destiny should be more than what happened to me. I wanted to make it so. My determination helped shape my future.

I first had to overcome the complacency instilled in me by both mom and dad. After high school, and the trip to Philadelphia, I found a job at a local company in Omaha. I worked data entry, going up the ladder from a part-time worker to department manager. For a young bachelor, having good money, a full-time job with health and retirement benefits and PTO was a new world to me. It hit me. At 20 years of age I had a better job than either of my parents ever obtained. I worked at the same company until I was 25, when I became burned out in the corporate world. There was plenty of room to grow within the company. It just didn't motivate me. It took time to realize motivation had to come from within.

One day in June 2011, with the help of a good friend, I started an unpaid internship at KVNO radio in Omaha. It was a small public radio station. They had me writing one sport story per week. It was refreshing. I took radio classes throughout high school. I was a natural. From those days of written sports recaps of games at grandma's house to calling in scores to our local sports radio station – I knew this was what I was destined to do. In October of 2011, I quit my corporate job and got a new one as a part-time news anchor at KVNO. Later, I was hired as a reporter and became the news director in 2013 and 2016 on an interim basis. I had no college degree, so it would only be temporary. Then I took the advice of a friend and went to college, starting at a community college in Omaha. By 2016, I enrolled at the University of Nebraska at Omaha, coincidentally, where KVNO studios are located.

On a whim in July of 2017, just before my senior year in college, I applied for a job as a morning radio host for Nebraska's NPR statewide radio network. It was a hosting and reporter job. I didn't think I had a shot, but didn't want to pass up on the chance to work at one of the truly great institutions in the state. After a lengthy interview process, I got the job. This is easily the highlight of my professional career (so far). I get to wake up every morning and spend time with my favorite people: Nebraskans. I also get to also tell in depth stories you don't hear anywhere else.

My past and trauma gives me perspective you don't always get from other journalists. When telling a story about poverty, foster care, the public school system and the like, I have personal insight.

I'm the luckiest guy in the state, having to pinch myself somedays, knowing they pay me for a job I'd do for free.

***

I have much to be thankful for and too many people to thank. I went to six different elementary schools in seven years: Pinewood, Walnut Hill, Wakonda, Minne Lusa, Dundee and Florence. I went to four junior high schools: McMillan, Norris, Bryan and Monroe.

That's 10 schools in 9 years.

I was hardly able to gain traction in one school before being taken out and shoved into another. Making friends was hard for me and keeping them was even harder.

Finally, in high school I found some scholastic stability going to Benson, where I graduated in 2004. Being able to stay in one school for four years had an impact I didn't necessarily notice at the time. Looking back, it was much needed.

There were people like my paternal grandfather, who had immeasurable impact on me. His impression on me in undeniable – from the hours I keep (waking early, napping in late afternoon) to my mannerisms (singing opera when alone).

Then there were surrogates like Mr. Earnhardt, a high school science teacher, a hard edged, no-nonsense kind of guy that I needed.

Working at Benson High School in Omaha in the early 2000s, a teacher had to be just as tough as the students or they'd be eaten up and spat out. Mr. E was a good man in every sense of the word. He never let students get away with anything. I was once three seconds (if that) late to his class – he was having none of it.

"If you show up late for your flight and you see your plane in the air as you arrive, do you think the airline workers will message the pilots to return the plane?"

This was rhetorical, of course. So, too, was his line about trying to help Benson students learn:

"You can lead a Benson student to knowledge, but you can't make them think."

Other surrogate parents I had over the years included Mrs. Tonnies (2nd grade at Pinewood) who put up with my rambunctiousness, Mrs. Shepherd (4th grade at Dundee) who offered a nurturing presence when I needed it, and Mr. Kennedy (A former Husker football captain in the 1960s, who got me interested in science at McMillan Jr High).

As a freshman at Benson, I lucked out. I had Mr. Shipley, who taught English and fed my love for 80s rock music by exchanging our favorite song lyrics in class, and Mr. Behrens who literally paid for my ticket to junior prom. He also paid for my tuxedo and gave me a bunch of his clothes during my junior year. Before grandpa died, he and grandma made sure we had everything we needed – school supplies like notebooks, backpacks, markers and crayons as well as several sets of clothes before school started. After grandpa died, we didn't have that safety net. So Mr. B's clothes were a godsend to me. I still have and wear the leather jacket he gave me, more than 15 years later.

Mr. Behrens also took me to my first Nebraska football game in 2002. It was the McNeese State football game where Jammal Lord broke the individual single game total yardage record for Nebraska. Mr. B knew of my love for the Huskers and he brought me to the Cornhusker state cathedral.

These people worked as teachers, all with their own lives and families and problems to live and deal with. Yet, they all gave of themselves to help me and I know they helped other students just like me.

That said, there were many other teachers who helped accidently, all of whom I met before high school. Being a transient student, as hard as it was for me to make friends, it also made it tough for teachers to connect with me. I had one teacher who was annoyed by my actions in her class at Norris Jr. High (7th grade) tell me:

"Brandon, you're not smart. You're a loser and you'll never amount to anything worthwhile."

The kids in class laughed at her retort.

Little did the teacher know the impact of this would last long. What she said angered me. But more than anything – I wanted to show her she was mistaken. I've taken that feeling with me throughout my life, the feeling of doubt from others. I use it as fuel, a sort of motivation to prove them wrong. While putting this book together, it's what drove me to write when I didn't think I had it in me.

By accepting my own accomplishments, I came to the realization that what we do with our story is much more important and interesting that what happened to us. We're shaped by our experiences but judged by what we do with them. Instead of pushing blame, I've found an outlet to prove naysayers wrong.

***

You may have gotten the idea that my life was nothing but a tragedy. My life *was* a tragedy, up and until I decided to change it. Life is a bunch of random circumstances, from who your parents are to when and where you are born. In the end, it's we who write our destinies.

I knew all those years ago in that small room in the youth shelter. I was imprisoned there by the state – unable to leave the building without being escorted by guards. I couldn't turn to any adult in my life and I couldn't escape to school. School would've at least been a place for me to breathe and take my mind off my reality. I focused my attention inward, like many do in similar situations. Instead of taking it and blaming the world, I chose to use it to better myself.

Sure, I was an angry kid, but I found outlets to discharge that energy. I turned to music, to the Huskers and later, to God. I was saved by my Lord and Savior, Jesus Christ in high school. His guidance and love as well as the church's fellowship got me out of deep trouble. I attended youth groups, Bible studies, church pot lucks, football Saturdays – all through church. It kept me out of drugs and trouble in high school. I realized that I had to forgive myself for all that my father did to me. His actions were his, but the blame I put on myself, was my doing.

It's easy to turn on the world, to become a cynic. Some people let the terrible things that happen to them ruin how they treat the world. We can become the harshness we've experienced. That is the real fight in life, to forgive those who've wronged us. Forgiveness is my release. It broke the chains that held me down. The best thing I did was give up the bitter pill of hatred and resentment. That's the burden on all of us, to look in the mirror and accept what we see and let go.

Sometimes the cure to your pain lies inside you. You may feel alone, like you're the only person who feels like you do. I can promise you that you aren't. There are countless people out there just like you who are suffering from the trauma of their childhood. It's easy to blame yourself for what happened. This only leads to further hurt and disappointment.

The most important step in any journey is that first step. Once you take that leap of faith, it gives you the strength to know you *can* continue on. Setting goals is important, so too is setting yourself up to attain them. Forgetting your past, burying it, not focusing on it – none of that will solve any of your pain.

It comes down to the resentment eating me alive. I had to give it up, to let go. Otherwise I'd be wasting decades seething at my past. Forgiveness isn't for the forgiven. It isn't about the person you're forgiving. It's about moving on and wanting to use your past to better your own situation. You can't change what happened to you, but it's not about undoing the past. It's about taking a stand.

If you hold it in for the rest of your life, they win. Those that hurt you don't care about what they've done. Continuing to blame them and holding grudges forever lets them win. You'll never forget them, but you have to stop letting them hurt you now. This is something I wish I would've known all those years ago.

It's taken me about twenty years of wallowing in the thick, drippy, molasses-like sludge of resentment to fully understand this. I've been rolling around in it long enough. I grew tired and wanted to show the world.

Understand what happened to you isn't fair, but also recognize that you alone can take the first step necessary to start the healing process. That can be reaching out and speaking to a therapist, a friend, or even to a Reddit support group for help.

Most importantly, what you suffered through isn't your fault. In the end, forgiveness is the answer – both forgiving your abusers and yourself. The way in to the abuse, I've found is the way out. We mustn't dodge our past and hide in shame. Instead we should face our fears head on.

Find your inner peace of mind and understand just as W.B. Yeats, the old Irish poet, said: happiness isn't about finding virtue or pleasure, but it's simply about growth. We are happy when we are growing. My true purification came from accepting that the past is best controlled when we break ties with it.

Out of the night that covers me,

Black as the pit from pole to pole,

I thank whatever gods may be

For my unconquerable soul.

In the fell clutch of circumstance

I have not winced nor cried aloud.

Under the bludgeonings of chance

My head is bloody, but unbowed.

Beyond this place of wrath and tears

Looms but the Horror of the shade,

And yet the menace of the years

Finds and shall find me unafraid.

It matters not how strait the gate,

How charged with punishments the scroll,

I am the master of my fate,

I am the captain of my soul.

-William Ernest Henley

Made in the USA
Las Vegas, NV
24 November 2020